ASI ES

Así Es

Stories of Hispanic Spirituality

Yolanda Tarango, C.V.V.I.
Ada María Isasi-Díaz
Consuelo Covarrubias, P.B.V.M.
Marco Antonio López Saavedra
Ricardo Ramírez, C.S.B.
María Teresa Gastón Witchger
Olga Villa Parra
Juan Sosa
Confesor De Jesús
Dominga M. Zapata
Silvia Zaldívar
José and Mercedes Rivera
Enrique D. Alonso
Alvaro Dávila
Clotilde Olvera Márquez

Arturo Pérez
Consuelo Covarrubias, P.B.V.M.
Edward Foley, Capuchin
Editors

Translated by Sarah C. Pruett
and Elena Sánchez Mora

A Liturgical Press Book

THE LITURGICAL PRESS
Collegeville, Minnesota

Cover design by Fred Petters.

Cover illustration: Detail, "Christ Crucified," School of Beneto, Orlega II, ca. 1875–1907.

1   2   3   4   5   6   7   8   9

Library of Congress Cataloging-in-Publication Data

Así es : stories of Hispanic spirituality / Yolanda Tarango . . . [et al.] ; Consuelo Covarrubias, Arturo Pérez, Edward Foley, editors ; translated by Sarah C. Pruett and Elena Sánchez Mora.
    p.   cm.
  ISBN 0-8146-2290-9
  1. Hispanic American Catholics—Religious life. 2. Catholic Church—United States—Membership. 3. Spirituality—United States—History—20th century. [1. Spirituality—Catholic Church—History—20th century.] I. Tarango, Yolanda.
  BX1407.H55A86   1994
  282'.73'08968—dc20   93-47029
                                          CIP

Contents

Introduction

Various saintly people have offered their paths to holiness for our edification and inspiration. Their lives of faith, along with their writings, journals, rules, and spiritual exercises can be called "schools of spirituality." From these schools we, the saints in process, are taught to discern our path to holiness. Besides these well recognized schools of spirituality, however, there are other "schools." It is often said that the "school of life" teaches far more effectively than any other. It is with our first breath that we begin to learn about life and about its Author. It is with our dying sigh that we master the lessons of living. The teachings of this school are not found in any book, rule, or structure but rather in the daily life encounters and experiences with our families, friends, neighbors, and, yes, enemies. Let us look at the stories of this other "school."

Spiritual stories

Hector

The distance between his house and the church was not very much, a few blocks at most. Hector, a young man of twenty, made the walk daily. Upon entering the church he would bless himself with holy water, as he had been taught since childhood. Turning left he walked a few more steps and knelt before the shrine of the crucified Lord. Since he first arrived in *el norte* Hector spent the beginning moments of every day seeking from this bloodied God a blessing on his efforts, on his family, and on his unfulfilled dreams. It was a simple ritual—ordinary and holy. *Así es.*

Raquel and Beto

The baby's stirrings woke Raquel who instantly was at her first born's crib. Hunger pains were the reason for the baby's early morning movements. Raquel sat down on the bed's edge, contradicting the saying "that you can't do two things at the same time." While nursing the infant, she began to awaken Beto from his peaceful sleep. They needed to be at the church by 9:00 in order "to present" their child and receive the priest's blessing. This blessing would protect them from the *mal de ojo* and any other evil. Beto's arm lovingly drew both mother and child closer to him. *Así es.*

Ana

Being a single woman in her late twenties was not a "tradition" in Ana's family, but Ana was never traditional. With all due respect to her parents, she lived her own life, balancing between what they thought she should do and what she knew she had to do. For the past year she had searched deep into her heart and heard the silence, the gentle breeze, and the voice of love calling. With the help of Sister Miriam, Ana had come to hear more and more clearly the invitation to live a vowed religious life. She would tell her parents tonight, after dinner. There were no "religious" in her family. She would be the first. Ana would continue to live untraditionally. *Así es.*

Oscar

"What's happening?" was the familiar phrase of all the dudes. Afro American, Mexican, and Puerto Rican young men would greet each other the same way. They were all born in this "hood." They knew its streets and alleys, dead-ends and hiding places. Oscar was a "happening" kind of guy, alive to the moment, to the crew with whom he partied, and to the life and death that surrounded him. He knew English better than he knew Spanish, and he knew street talk better than he knew English. He went to the 11:00 Mass almost every Sunday—when he got up. He and his friends always stood in the back of the church by the center door. It was reserved for the party crew. They bothered no one and no one bothered them. *Así es.*

Así es colloquially means "that's the way things are." There is no implicit judgement upon "the things" in the phrase— just a simple statement of life summarizing the moment, the event, the fact, or the reality. These few words express a practical philosophy of life. For someone who does not understand Hispanic ways and, therefore, the Hispanic person, the phrase may seem to depict passivity, ambivalence, or tolerance of the status quo. For the Hispanic person, the *dicho* (saying) may be an act of faith, a statement of trust, or an act of resignation to the will of God. Our concern is to look at the "way things are" in the spiritual life from the Hispanic perspective. What has the school of life taught us about God?

First, it is valuable to reflect upon the nature of "spirituality" and second, to discover how it is translated and incarnated in the lives of Hispanic[1] people. As vague and personal as the subject of spirituality is, there have been scholarly tomes, dictionaries, and encyclopedias written about it. Henri Nouwen, Joann Wolski Conn, Anne Carr, and Thomas Merton are authors who often reflect and write about spirituality from the perspective of the school of life. Their popularity comes from the fact that everyone can see themselves in their spiritual writings. The writings of Ricardo Ramírez, Rosa María Icaza, and Allan Figueroa Deck[2] are a special point of reference for us. The articles by these writers are some of the only writings that treat the topic of Hispanic spirituality. They are touchstones in our learning.

Spirituality is like a prism refracting light in a multitude of directions. Each refraction is true; each refraction is different. The Holy Spirit is the authentic source of this light—glowing in diverse ways within us. There are no limits here, no proper or correct ways of coming to know God or of responding to the Spirit's playfulness and initiatives. C.P.M. Jones wisely states, "In spirituality, there are ultimately no 'rules of the game,' even those laid down by the saints, but only 'tips of the trade,' freely offered to be freely available to those who need them."[3] It is up to us to decide when and how to use these tips. We encounter the Spirit on the playground of our hearts and so are drawn closer to God. To be drawn closer to God is the ultimate goal and the focus of any "school of spirituality."

How might we define spirituality? We need to articulate a definition not for the purpose of restricting spirituality within some tight knit statement. Rather we are motivated to define spirituality in order to become more conscious of the common, holy ground on which we stand. This in turn influences the way we speak, make decisions, prioritize our day, choose our friends, and celebrate our faith. In effect spirituality is both a conscious and unconscious, habitual and unintentional God-presence that gives meaning to our lives. An authentic spirituality is woven into the fabric of our Christian existence.

Robert Schreiter enunciates four very helpful characteristics of spirituality:

1. Spirituality is the expression of the Christian meaning of our lives as individuals and in communities . . . (it) needs to be explicit—that is, expressed in outward form and words.
2. Spirituality is rooted in a distinctive understanding of the gospel of Jesus Christ. . . . This allows one to build a focus and center in one's life and one's relationship to God.
3. Spiritualities are concrete and express themselves more in images than in concepts. As contrasted with theologies in the strict sense, spiritualities are concerned with the concrete tasks of daily living in a specific context. . . . They are concerned with concepts, but mainly as to how concepts are translated or applied to a specific problem or situation. For that reason, they are more often expressed in images or embodied in exemplary individuals than in conceptual categories.
4. Spirituality is rooted in both Christian tradition and contemporary experience. . . . Because of this double rootage, authentic Christian spirituality neither incorporates all contemporary experience into Christian tradition, nor does it accommodate the gospel to contemporary culture. It is instead a mutually critical and mutually correlative activity, whereby Christian tradition challenges the interpretation of our Christian experience, and contemporary experience challenges the way we interpret Christian tradition.[4]

In view of these characteristics, we can define Christian spirituality as a way of life that reveals, helps, and builds our relationship with God through the Good News of Jesus. Building a relationship with God is a life long work. This relationship is translated into human terms of coming to trust and be trusted, to hurt and to be hurt, to forgive and be forgiven, to love and be loved. At each turn there is a heartfelt decision that needs to be made: either to continue or to stop. There is a challenge to risk further for God. Hector, Raquel and Beto, Ana, and Oscar are all engaged in building a relationship with the God of their lives. They do this as individuals but also as members of the Hispanic community that is itself gifted by God with religious traditions. These traditions are the religious heritage of the Hispanic community. They form the contemporary religious experience of this people. These traditions are expressed in what is commonly called *Religiosidad Popular* (popular religiosity).[5] This is a part of the school of life, the school of spirituality for and from the Hispanic community. These expressions are transforming experiences of grace that constantly change and challenge us in our desire to be drawn closer to God.

In 1985 Bishop Ricardo Ramírez wrote about spirituality from the Hispanic perspective. He described spirituality as the inner space that allows people to come in touch with themselves as believers. It is the area where "the divine spirit touches the human spirit." Specifically referring to Hispanics he states:

> For Hispanics, this faith experience that is at the heart of spirituality touches not only the spiritual . . . but is also one that affects their total lives . . . it brings (Hispanic) people in touch with the past spirituality of their ancestors.[6]

Ramírez himself states that this is more a description than a definition of Hispanic spirituality.

Rosa María Icaza's article "Spirituality of the Mexican American People"[7] employs a definition influenced by the National Pastoral Plan for Hispanic Ministry.[8] "Spirituality is the orientation and perspective of all dimensions of a person's life in the following of Jesus, moved by the Spirit, and in continuous dialogue with the Father." The human context for spelling out such a definition of spirituality is clarified by Icaza when she cites the guidelines of the III Encuentro that "express their concern for family, the poor, youth, and women; their desire for education/culture, justice, missionary action, and leadership; and their need to be part of its planning and implementation."[9] She concludes: "It seems then, that for Hispanics, spirituality is translated into the love of God, which moves, strengthens and is manifested in love of neighbor and self."[10] She goes on to specify eight characteristics taken from the National Pastoral Plan that describe Hispanic spirituality.[11] Although the National Pastoral Plan does attempt to characterize the spirituality of all Hispanic groups, Icaza's article seems to focus solely on the Mexican American experience. This raises many questions regarding other Hispanic ethnic groups and their spiritualities. We can wonder, "What are their similarities and differences?" "What are the nuanced characteristics of these spiritual forces?"

Allan Figueroa Deck notes very clearly that the term "Hispanic" is an umbrella term that must be treated with caution.

> Any generalized understanding must be complemented by more detailed analysis of the particular group one is dealing with. The most salient points in common among the vast and diverse groups are the Spanish language and their particular brand of Catholicism produced beginning in the sixteenth century in the Americas.[12]

Deck directs our attention to the fact that Hispanics only exist in the United States. In their countries of origin they are the citizens of those particular national territories, for example Colombians in Colombia are not Hispanics, nor are Guatemalans in Guatemala. For better or for worse, in crossing the United States border, they do not lose their national heritage but rather take on the economic, sexual, racial, ethnic, religious, and cultural experiences of the Hispanics already living here. Some may see this as a creative tension, while others may experience more the anxiety of living in two worlds. All Hispanic ethnic groups come into contact not only with one another but also with the larger multi-racial, multi-cultural society. These are strong influences shaping and forming a person's spirituality.

Ramírez, Icaza, and Deck include the practices of popular religiosity as fundamental and expressive of Hispanic spirituality. Yet there is a further question that arises here. Although, for example, we have begun to move from the understanding that a sarape on an altar is not Hispanic liturgy, have we yet moved from a *description* of Hispanic spirituality as popular religiosity to an understanding of its uniqueness as a school of spirituality? This is difficult since spirituality is more a matter of the heart than of the head, more a matter of faith than a matter of logic. Our challenge is a bit like trying to hold water in our hands. Yet we must try, in order to better appreciate and affirm the gifts God has given to us.

We have chosen to explore the nature of Hispanic spirituality through real stories that make up the chapters of this book. Each woman and man writes from the genius of their particular Hispanic ethnic group and from their particular vocation in life. This is an exercise in *teología de conjunto*, a way of theologizing together from one another's faith experiences. From the *conjunto* of these stories we hope to discern more clearly and faithfully God's work within the Hispanic community.

Through the stories and reflections of the writers of this book, we can identify the "sacred ground" on which we as a Hispanic people walk. We believe that there is a uniqueness, a charism, a true gift that allows us to know God in the particular ways of our various ethnic groups as well as in the bonds of a heritage that hold us together as a Hispanic community. Our hope is that this book will serve as a reference point for those who minister, Hispanic and non-Hispanic alike, within the Hispanic community so that together we might "have the strength to grasp the breadth and the length, the height and the depth, until knowing the love of Christ, which is beyond all knowledge, (we) are filled with the utter fullness of God" (Eph 3:18-19).

Así es!

Arturo Pérez, Consuelo Covarrubias, P.B.V.M.,
Edward Foley, Capuchin
October 12, 1992

NOTES

1. The term "Hispanic" refers to the people of Latin American origin who reside in the United States. See Allan Figueroa Deck, *The Second Wave* (New York: Paulist Press, 1989) 5.

2. Ricardo Ramírez, "Hispanic Spirituality," *Social Thought* (Summer 1985) 6-13. Rosa María Icaza, "Spirituality of the Mexican American," *Worship* 63 (1989) 232-246. Allan Figueroa Deck, "The Spirituality of the United States Hispanic: An Introductory Essay," *U.S. Catholic Historian* 9 (1990) 137-146.

3. C.P.M. Jones, "Liturgy and Personal Devotion," *The Study of the Liturgy*, ed. Cheslyn Jones, Geoffrey Wainwright, Edward Yarnold (New York: Oxford University Press, 1986) 6.

4. Robert Schreiter, *In Water and Blood* (New York: Crossroad, 1988) 131-32.

5. Arturo Pérez, *Popular Catholicism* (Washington: Pastoral Press, 1988) 7.

6. Ramírez, 6.

7. Icaza, 232.

8. "Spirituality is understood to be the way of life of a people, a movement by the Spirit of God, and the grounding of one's identity as a Christian in every circumstance of life. It is the struggle to live the totality of one's personal and communitarian life in keeping with the Gospel; spirituality is the orientation and perspective of all the dimensions of a person's life in the following of Jesus and in continuous dialogue with the Father." *National Pastoral Plan for Hispanic Ministry* (Washington: United States Catholic Conference, 1987) 7.

9. Icaza, 232.

10. Ibid.

11. Icaza gleans from the National Pastoral Plan the following characteristics of Hispanic spirituality:

> 1. A basic and constant aspect is a sense of the presence of God.
> 2. God is found in the arms of the Virgin Mary. She is at the heart of their spirituality.
> 3. "The seeds of the Word" in pre-Hispanic cultures are still cultivated.
> 4. Spirituality is expressed in popular devotions and in the use of symbols and gestures.
> 5. It is also expressed in behavior regarding gospel values, such as prayer and hospitality, endurance and hope, commitment and forgiveness.
> 6. Faith is kept alive at home through practices in daily life and particularly during the principal seasons of the liturgical year.

7. All celebrations are seen as communal and most of them include prayer, sharing of food, and singing/dancing/reciting or composing poetry.

8. Finally, Hispanics seldom pray for themselves but regularly for others. They often request others to remember them in their prayers.

12. Deck, 138.

1

A Hispanic Woman's "Spirituality"

Yolanda Tarango, C.V.V.I.

My experience as a Hispanic woman and my conversations with other Hispanic women suggest that the term "spirituality" is not often used. This does not mean that Hispanic women are not deeply faithful Christians committed to growing in holiness. It does, however, indicate that the concept of "spirituality" is not a familiar or comfortable one. The very term conveys a dichotomy between the spiritual and the material. This is a foreign concept in Hispanic culture where religion pervades every aspect of life. As Hispanics, we ordinarily do not separate the spiritual from the material life. Our tendency is to see all life as a whole and holy.

Peruvian theologian Gustavo Gutiérrez talks about the spirituality of the minorities to describe the dominance of monastic religious thinking in the Christian community's understanding of spirituality. A way of relating to God that has been accessible to only a minority of the Christian community has been validated as the only way to God and enjoined on the majority of Christians. If prayer is presumed to take place within the spiritual versus the material realm of life then spirituality is reduced to a state of consciousness rather than a way of living. This not only removes it from the grasp of the ordinary Christian but also invalidates their experience of meeting God in the daily events of life. The very use of the term spirituality reinforces the bias toward dualistic thinking.

Those of us who are Hispanic members of religious congregations, or who have studied in seminaries, have been schooled in dualistic Eurocentric concepts of prayer and spirituality. If we are to understand religious experience in the Hispanic context, we need to touch our own early experience of faith and to reclaim the religious understandings conveyed to us by our families. It is only in this way that we can begin to challenge the framework into which all religious experience has been forced to fit.

I believe that in order to comprehend how Hispanic women understand their relationship with God, and its implications for their daily lives, we need to change some of our assumptions as well as our language. For this reason, I will use the term "religious experience" rather than "spirituality" in this essay. I believe it is a more appropriate term when talking about Hispanic women's understanding of living in relationships with God.

Perhaps the first clue to speaking of our religious experience is to *describe* not *define*. Hispanic women tend to speak about God and their relationships with God, not in abstract concepts, but with examples of faith-filled people. The following examples, from conversations with Hispanic women, exemplify this:

> My grandmother was a very religious woman. In the family she was the epitome of faith, the epitome of religion. And that was so not only in my family but in the community and that is still true. My first memory of praying is of going with grandmother to visit people in the community. She helped others, went to be with others.[1]

> In a very special way I have to mention an uncle of mine. He never married; he was blind in one eye and saw just a little out of the other. In the house my mother had an altar, my grandmother had an altar . . . and when this uncle would wake up, the first thing he would do was pray. The example my grandmother, my mother, this uncle gave me was having faith in God. They always hoped that one day it would be better for us. Maybe they would not see those better times, but the younger ones would.[2]

If I want to learn about a Hispanic woman's religious experience I might begin by asking, "¿Quién es la persona más santa que conoces?'' (''Who is the most saintly or holiest person you know?'') More often than not, that person will be the woman's mother, grandmother or relative. The description of how that person lived and the example they gave is usually an indication of the individual's own beliefs about what characterizes a relationship with God and its expression in daily life. In the two examples above we hear these women saying that the relationship with God is characterized by service to others and is lived in a spirit of hope.

Another earmark of religious experience for Hispanic women is that *feeling* takes primacy over knowing or thinking. What is important in describing religious experience is not ''insight'' about God but rather the feelings that are elicited when you have experienced God's presence:

> I have never thought of describing God because for me it is not a person, it is like a *sentimiento* (deep feeling), a force that makes me move, which pushes me in difficult moments. It is a force, something I cannot explain.[3]

> I have never doubted God, that I remember. Any moment, wherever I am, *siento* (I feel) his presence. If I see a person in need, my heart aches, it hurts inside me.[4]

I believe that the emphasis on feeling is reflective of the intimacy that people experience in the presence of God. Furthermore, it is ''feeling'' that awakens consciousness and recognition of the presence of God, especially in those who suffer. In the two statements above, these Hispanic women experience the presence of God as a force that strengthens them to face difficult moments and as a call to solidarity with those in need.

In describing my own religious experience, my starting point is always my grandmother. I remember her as the one who introduced me to the church and who let me walk by her side as she told me stories of faith and endurance. She had a hard life which included being orphaned at three years of age and widowed at twenty-three.

She was pulled out of elementary school in order to stay home and assist an invalid step-mother; later, she worked as a maid, cook and cafeteria worker to support her children. In spite of this history, what characterized her was not bitterness but an insatiable ability to love. This was expressed in her care-giving and her compassion. The *Virgen de Guadalupe* was her best and closest friend; there was not a thing she didn't dis-cuss with her. In return, *Guadalupe* gave her comfort and ac-companied her in difficult times. When I decided to join the convent my grandmother was not happy at all and, as she con-fessed many years later, she even tried to discourage me. She was afraid that the lifestyle would rob me of happiness. How-ever, after visiting me in the convent and seeing that I was happy, she went back and apologized to *la Virgen*. My grand-mother was always close to the church. She went to daily Mass and said endless rosaries. Yet, she was always ready and happy to do for others. Whether she was attending Mass or serving others, it was all in the name of God. From her I learned that loving God is loving and forgiving others, pure and simple; that is all that is expected of us. When she was slowed down with age and could not offer service to others, her gift was her presence. In her later years, until she died, I think of her as simple goodness. Just to be with her was a gift. She left me with an image of God as grandmother, with open arms, ready to draw me into her embrace.

When I joined the convent, I was introduced to the con-cept of spiritual exercises. These were rational activities to strengthen the spiritual life. The daily prayer regimen included meditation, introspective self-evaluations, and recitation of prayers. For years I tried to be faithful to this prescription for nurturing the relationship with God, but somehow it never seemed to be enough. I never really *felt* like I was praying, or praying enough. I was constantly working at being more prayerful and expecting that all the effort had to be on my part.

One summer I found myself in a retreat house in Cuerna-vaca, Mexico, that seemed the perfect environment for prayer. It was peaceful and quiet and had beautiful gardens. Further-more, I had time to pray; I had no excuse. Yet, I would walk through the garden, and I would sit in the balcony, and I would go to the chapel, but I just could not "pray." I was constantly struggling with distractions. Finally, one morning I was so frus-trated, I decided to give up and go for a walk instead. As soon as I stepped outside by the large gates, I saw a man bent over carrying a huge burden. I *felt* badly and I knew I had just met God. I walked a little further and I saw a woman with a child on her back and two others hanging from her skirt. This also elicited feelings of pain and sadness and, again, I knew I had met God suffering. All the way to town I kept seeing the face of God in the faces and suffering of those I passed. I felt deeply moved and I realized that I had been praying all the way. It dawned on me that I spent all those years trying to pray in a way that was totally foreign to me. No wonder I had so much difficulty, I had distrusted my own experience.

I realized that I had limited myself to what I had been taught about prayer and I had closed myself off to the many other ways that God spoke to me. That was an important lesson for me because I began to understand how prayer had been dichotomized and privatized, which had not only limited my understanding of prayer but also invalidated the way the majority of Christians pray. No wonder so many people had come to doubt their own ability to pray and thought that only the nuns and the priests really prayed. I, myself, had learned to give more importance to institutionalized prayer than to my own experience and to the wisdom of my grandmother.

I am conscious that the way I pray is by being in the presence of God's people, especially the suffering and dispossessed. My concept of the appropriate place of prayer has changed as well. I live in a shelter with homeless women and children and that is my church—my place of prayer. The first challenge was to identify where I meet God most naturally and then to trust this experience. In doing so, I also validate what I learned from my grandmother. I recognized that the way prayer has been appropriated and institutionalized by a male religious minority is by dichotomizing reality and putting religious experience in the sphere of the private. Prayer has been portrayed as a God-and-me relationship. This individualistic approach, especially for Hispanic women, is in conflict with the communal piety of loving devotion with which we have been brought up.

In essence, I believe that Hispanic women's religious experience is characterized less by pious practices and holy thoughts and more by a piety of concrete acts of love and justice.

NOTES

1. Ada María Isasi-Díaz and Yolanda Tarango, C.V.V.I., *Hispanic Women—Prophetic Voice in the Church* (San Francisco: Harper & Row, 1988) 28.

2. Ibid., 40.

3. Ibid., 16.

4. Ibid., 23.

2

To Struggle for Justice Is to Pray

Ada María Isasi-Díaz

Introduction

In October 1967 I was invited to walk in the place of honor in a procession through a very poor *barriada* on the outskirts of Lima, Peru, where I was working. The place of honor was immediately in front of the image of *El Señor de Los Milagros*, facing it.[1] This meant I had to walk backwards! For the long hours of the procession (it went on into a second day!), I watched people praying in front of the image, offering flowers and candles to *El Señor*. Barefooted women walked next to me in fulfillment of promises they had made. Little children were lifted on high and touched to the image. The procession stopped repeatedly at elaborate altars decorated with flowers and candles constructed in front of very poor homes. Not until much later did I realize the deep meaning this experience was to have for me.

At the time I was a member of a canonical religious community. Working in this parish was my first assignment. Full of the best of intentions, I worked very hard; I wanted to win souls for Jesus, to help people be good Catholics! I had seen my work with those in charge of the procession as a wonderful avenue to instruct them about the teachings of our Church, about the Catholic faith they claimed as their own. My "missionary" mindset had already been challenged and my "missionary" zeal had been somewhat curbed by liberation theology that was beginning to flourish at that time in Lima. My spiritual director had advised me to spend my first year

16

in Lima listening. "Go to meetings and listen; in church, listen to women as they pray out loud in front of the statues; listen to students as they evaluate their retreats and projects." The sense of the "privilege of the poor" was beginning to become a grounding principle for me.

As I walked home after the procession, I realized how privileged I was to have been part of such an outpouring of faith—the faith of the poor and the oppressed that maintains them, that is their sustenance in the most trying of situations. I felt that my well-reasoned faith, a so-called sophisticated faith illumined by the "right" kind of theology, was not any deeper or any more pleasing to God than the faith of the poor people I had seen expressed for two days. In the weeks that followed I came to realize more and more the depth of that faith. I came to understand that their lack of sophistication in explaining and expressing faith does *not* mean that their faith was shallow. Perhaps the most important learning from the experience was that I came to trust the religious understandings and practices of the poor and the oppressed. Ever since then, I have accepted their religiosity as part of the ongoing revelation of God in our world—in my life.

Self-Sacrifice + Prayer = Holiness?

Recently I found a letter I had written to my parents the first month I was in the novitiate. In it I described the "holiness" of one of the older novices whom I admired greatly. As I read what I had written, I remembered the deep desire I had then to be holy. At that time, holiness in the convent was defined in terms of self-sacrifice and long hours of meditation and prayer. As a nineteen-year-old, I struggled to be close to God by doing what those in authority told me to do. But it was to no avail. I did not feel closer to God; I could not convince myself that I was a terrible sinner; I could not see any reason for flagellating myself; I could not see any reason for thinking I had failed terribly when I fell asleep in chapel during meditation at 5:30 in the morning.[2]

The more I heard about the spiritual life, saving one's soul, the life of prayer, holiness and spirituality, the more I thought that the convent was not the place where I was supposed to be. I also began to wonder what "spirituality" really meant or who, besides the nuns, ever used the word. For example, I did not remember my mother, one of the strongest influences in my life, ever talking about spirituality. Little by little I began to realize that the word "spirituality" was often used to set the nuns and priests apart from and above others.

In those novitiate years the more I failed to become "spiritual" the more I became convinced that God was calling me to minister among the poor. Since all the messages I received about not being "spiritual" enough did not shake this conviction, I began to question the meaning of "spirituality." Much later I came to realize that what I could not accept was the false notion that the soul is a separate entity, that one can counterpose body and spirit as if the human person could be split in two.

My discomfort with the word "spirituality" and the way it is still commonly used only grew as I finished my years of training and was assigned to work in Peru. Spirituality, for the majority of nuns and priests, continued to be equated with prayer, meditation, and penance. Furthermore, I was advised repeatedly that these practices were to feed my ministry. Coming to believe in the ongoing revelation of God in the struggle for survival of the poor and the oppressed only complicated things for me. Were the poor and the oppressed not holy because they did not pray formally every day? Were those who prayed long hours, did penance and meditated more pleasing to God than the majority of people who did not even go to Mass every Sunday?

Though I was not to articulate it until years later, it was then that I began to realize that the lived experience of the poor and the oppressed was to be the source of my theology, the grounding for what I believe about God, and the basis for understanding what God asks of me. I became aware that they were too busy struggling for food, a roof over their heads, and medicine for their children to worry about saving their souls. Their daily undertaking to find bodily sustenance parallels the original "give us this day our daily bread."

I Pray Best by Working for Justice

Since those days in Peru in the mid-1960s, I have understood myself as a justice-activist. Understanding that the oppression of Hispanic women is deeply rooted in patriarchy and the racist/ethnic prejudice so prevalent in this country has provided me with a point of entry into the struggle for liberation. What I do and who I am are greatly defined by this struggle. And I believe that my participation in the struggle for liberation is what helps me to become fully the person God intends me to be: a self I welcome, I like, I treasure.

As the years have gone by I have accepted that striving to live to the fullest by struggling against injustice is to draw nearer and nearer to the divine. Drawing closer to God and struggling for justice have become one and the same thing for me. Struggling for my liberation and the liberation of Hispanic women is a liberative praxis. This means that it is an activity both intentional and reflective; it is a communal praxis that feeds on the realization that Christ is among us when we strive to live the gospel message of justice and peace.

Following the example of grassroot Hispanic women, I do not think in terms of spirituality. But I know myself as a person with a deep relationship with the divine, a relationship that finds expression in walking picket lines more than in kneeling, in being in solidarity with the poor and the oppressed more than in fasting and mortifying the flesh, in striving to be passionately involved with others more than in being detached, in attempting to be faithful to who I am and what I believe God wants of me more than in following prescriptions for holiness that require me to negate myself.

NOTES

1. *El Señor de Los Milagros* is the main devotion in Peru. The image is the picture of the crucifixion, with the two Marys at the foot of the cross, and the hand of God the Father [sic] and the dove representing the Holy Spirit on top of the crucifix. The devotion started a long time ago when a wall with a fresco with the crucifixion was all that was left standing in a church after an earthquake. Millions participate every year

in the main procession. Almost every parish has its own procession. In the parish where I had been made *madrina* of the *Damas del Señor de Los Milagros* (the Ladies Auxiliary) I was often invited to assist at the meeting of the *Hermandad del Señor de Los Milagros* (the brotherhood in charge of the procession). Later that year I was made the *madrina* of one of the four squads of men who carry the image during the procession.

2. In an attempt to "check out reality" as I was seeing it, early on during my novitiate I ventured to ask some questions of Father Phillips, our extraordinary confessor who came once a month (we went to confession once a week with our ordinary confessor). Father Phillips had been a missionary in China and had survived three years of cruel imprisonment at the time of the communist revolution. I will always be indebted to him for helping me to see that there was nothing wrong with me for not understanding God's will and holiness the way others did!

3

"My Dear Mom"

Consuelo Covarrubias, P.B.V.M.

My dear Mom,

I was invited to write about my spirituality as a Hispanic religious. Even though you are no longer with me, it seems right that I share this with you, since your love and your values set the tone for my understanding of God. However, this short letter only allows my sharing a few of the key memories that helped shape my spirituality.

Spirituality is a way of life that reveals the sacred and cultivates the relationship with the sacred and the Holy One.[1] I live a Christian spirituality; it is nourished from my relationship with Jesus Christ. The "eyes" through which I learn about my God are identity and culture. Mom, you always told me I was *Mexicanita*. I asked "Why?" "Because" you responded "your papá and mamá are Mexicanos." Simple. You also taught us nine kids to pray and read in Spanish before we began first grade. Everyday we ate the ordinary simple Mexican fare set before us.

You taught me to know God in many ways throughout my childhood. As a preschooler I would stand on tiptoes to glimpse the altar that covered the top of the tall white dresser in your bedroom. A statue of the Blessed Mother stood in the middle surrounded by holy cards of your favorite saints and Our Lady of Guadalupe. Candles and a rosary guarded the front. Stacked on the side were the thumbworn, dogeared prayerbooks you and Dad used.

On some occasional quiet evening you would open the big trunk that filled the corner of the bedroom. For me, all things in it held a special awe. I liked it when you opened the green box with lots of pretty red, white, and green ribbons fixed up like little corsages with special buttons pinned on them. These buttons had the faces of our "heroes." I remember holding the one with Padre Hidalgo's picture on it. You told us he was the great man who led the people to victory during Mexico's war of independence and related little stories of how God and Our Lady of Guadalupe accompanied him. A cream colored box tied with a silk string kept your favorite photographs. You would talk about each person in the pictures. The stories revolved around the experiences of our relatives. You spoke about how God gifted, how God celebrated, and even how God would take care of the wrongdoers. God was big in your life, Mom, and for me God seemed vast. If the story was happy or funny, I imagined God as sunny, warm and friendly. If you told a sad story involving pain, I felt God as in a cloudy day. You picked up Abuelita's picture and related how you had to work after school, helping her prepare and serve meals for the men who worked in the gold mines. You spoke of the hazardous conditions and of the low wages they earned. You assured us that God would pay the unjust *patron* his dues and shower compassion on the people. I recall sensing God in darkness, removing evil and comforting the poor. Somehow I learned never to fear darkness because God was in it caring for those in need.

Mom, both your stories and your actions affected me. When we went to town you always greeted everyone you met in your broken English and spread warmth with your assuring smile. Everyone merited respect in your eyes, whether they were Anglos, Native Americans or our own people. I remember thinking to myself, "So this is what Mom means when she tells us that God wants us to love others."

In school, even my teachers seemed to challenge me to be clear on what God meant to me. In the fall of my senior year, one of my favorite teachers asked me what I planned to do with my life. I replied that I wanted to be a teacher like my older sister Mary, or a county agent like Hazel Thompson. Either way, I wanted to help people. The question jarred me.

During Lent of that year I made special visits at our parish church everytime we came into town. I would pray for my fiancé who was in the service, and I also pondered my teacher's question. "Planning my life" seemed to mean something broader than preparing for college or getting married. I asked God to help me figure this out so that I could have peace in my heart and a response for my teacher. I began to use some of those aspirations or mantras that you always whispered to yourself all day long like: "Alabado sea el santísimo, sacramento del altar, en los cielos, en la tierra y en todo lugar" and "Ayúdame Señor" (Praise be the Blessed Sacrament, in heaven, on the earth, and everywhere" and "Lord, help me"). I would say them inside of me, over and over like you did. By the time spring and the graduation ceremony and parties were over, I knew that "planning my life so that I could help people" meant involving God in a special way. One Saturday I went into the confessional to talk to the priest. I asked him to help me, because I wanted to become a sister.

Religious life was another step in deepening my relationship with God. My early formation days posed a challenging transition in this process. I didn't tell you about this, Mom, but the most difficult thing for me in the beginning was living a rigid schedule. It was like we read in Ecclesiastes 3: there was a time for rising, a time for eating, a time for studying, a time for doing chores, a time for recreating and a time for not recreating, a time for praying, a time for sleeping, a time for the Great Silence and I found a time for crying. I was homesick.

With the help of my novitiate companions, I soon became accustomed to living in a totally different world. I adjusted to the food and even to praying the Office. My whole existence at that time was planned so that I would be away from the real world. That was the spirituality of the time. I remember that as young professed sisters, Judy and I would sit by the classroom window watching people come out of Mass. When all of the people were gone, we'd go out for our walk. Thank God for Vatican II and the renewal of religious life. Wonderful, positive changes happened. We studied our history to rediscover the spirit and charism of our foundress in light of the times and the spirit of the Gospel. Now it is gratifying to come out of Sunday Mass with the people and stand there and visit with the parents of my students, just like ordinary folks. Soon the doors opened up for a broader interpretation of ministry.

In the early 1970s I began team teaching in the Milwaukee Public School Bilingual program. For the first time I made friends with other Hispanics and realized that I had lost much of my cultural identity. I felt angry, disappointed and cheated. As I grieved my loss I distanced myself from my religious community. I felt no one would comprehend my emptiness and pain; I couldn't even articulate it at the time. Fortunately for me, Mom, I received permission to do the thirty day Spiritual Exercises of St. Ignatius. This was the turning point of my life. Each day I experienced a different sense of God, especially during my walks in nature. The experience freed me to question whether I would even remain in religious life. I discovered that God would continue to love me regardless of my lifestyle. I was affirmed in my call to work with people, but this time I knew the focus must be with my Hispanic people. It would be from them that I would reclaim my cultural identity, with the *pueblo* where my language would become more facile and it was where I would discover new images of God and a new sense of Church. I think I wept for days. They were tears of peace and joy. I elected to remain in religious life and I also chose to be with those most in need. At that time I didn't know that I was making a preferential option for the poor. In time, after preparation at the Mexican American Cultural Center in San Antonio, Texas, and with full support from my congregation, I left the classroom and began Hispanic pastoral ministry.

Ministry was another facet of my life's journey that brought me face to face with my God through the people I accompanied and the circumstances of their lives. I learned that our God is a God that calls us to freedom. Jesus died that we might have life in abundance (John 10:10). I also discovered that one of the most wonderful gifts that I've received from God is the ability to use my talents in pastoral work to bring out some of that freedom. Mom, it is so good to see people become agents of change. They inquire, become involved, and soon are using their gifts, as they grow and take ownership of their small Christian communities, their volunteer work, their parish and even their civic communities. I remember you and Dad were some of the key organizers of the *fiestas patrias* in your time. Once you even brought to Montana the *Mexicanos* from the Denver symphony orchestra to perform on September 16. It highlighted our culture and brought good will to the community.

On occasions in my ministry I have been in situations where parts of it were not healthy or growthful. Then I have to make choices that are life giving. This stretches my ability to "let go." I recall that whenever you made plans or contemplated a new action you always added, "Si Dios nos da licencia" ("If God wills it"). That was one of your ways of letting go. I've discovered that my saying "Si Dios me da licencia" does not diminish the sadness and pain of having to uproot and leave the caring people with whom I have walked. I've learned to embrace the joyful memories as well as the pain. I've let the pain heal within as I continued my life's journey.

Mom, my spirituality in the broad sense is incarnational and ecclesial, whose source of meaning and life is Jesus Christ, but in a personal sense I find that the word journey seems to fit for me. Just as you and Dad journeyed from Mexico and came to a new land, knowing that God would always be at your side, I find myself on a journey in this country. I know that Jesus is my companion and that I am his follower, walking with others in community to build God's reign of freedom here on earth.

These short pieces of my life reveal only bits of my spiritual journey. My Hispanic roots and the charism of my congregation color the map of my life. Prayer and discernment are some of the foods that sustain me on my journey. My talents and gifts are the tools that help in building the reign of God. Special people have been the guides and special events the guideposts in my response to the sacred. I am grateful to my favorite high school teacher for provoking an initial discernment of my life, but I especially thank you, Mom, for teaching me my faith and grounding me in an experience of God through your stories and your own energetic and compassionate love for people. As I continue my spiritual journey, I know

I will count on you for help, not only for myself but for those with whom I walk. Thank you for being my Mom!

Your loving daughter,
Consuelo

NOTE

1. Classnotes from Spirituality 1 with Dr. Ed Sellner, College of St. Catherine, St. Paul, Minnesota, 1987.

4

The Well

Marco Antonio López Saavedra

Like most others, there are certain memories of my childhood that continue with me. Some of these are memories of
places, people, and practices. As a Mexican born in Chicago,
I spent time between Chicago and Mexico. In particular, two
years of my childhood were spent in San Luis Potosí where
my Mom was born and my father was raised. The earliest
memories of my childhood are from those two years and from
the house where my Mom and aunts had many memories
themselves. One of the things I remember is a well found in
the back patio of the house. I remember spending a lot of time
in that patio playing and doing the kind of things five-year-
old boys do. So often I felt that the well was in the way. It
kept my brother and I from extending our soccer game or it
always seemed to favor him since he could maneuver very well
around it and score on me before I could do anything about
it. Other times, as I rode my tricycle, I would pretend it was
a house that I was traveling around.

The well itself was very plain looking. It was not round or
made out of bricks but was rather a cement block with a cross
bar and an opening on top which was usually covered with
a metal plate. It was not often that I could look in to see how
deep it was or what was at the bottom. I never saw anyone
drawing water out of it, although I later found out that during
times of drought it proved to be important even for some of
the neighbors. To me, however, it seemed that people were
always pouring something into it such as the dirty mop water,

or water left over after washing the dishes or watering the plants. As I grew older, I also grew curious and would climb on top of it and yell to see if there was anyone down in the well. I was always very careful not to fall and would hold tightly to the crossbar or to a rope that occasionally hung from the crossbar. Sometimes I would drop some pebbles down into the well and I would hear a splash, but that was no indication of how much water there was. I sometimes thought about the well and at other times simply took it for granted and went about the business of enjoying life as a five-year-old. For better or for worse, there, in the center of what was my world, was this mysterious well which at times I wanted to know more about and at times I simply ignored.

Much like my experience of the well is my experience of spirituality. For most of my life, I seemed to think only of what I saw of the well and never gave much thought to its depth. At times the well, like my spirituality, was a wonderful part of my life and at others an obstruction or something I didn't want to deal with. Nevertheless, both the well and my spirituality have always been present. Further reflection has caused me to ask what is it that makes a well a well? The cement block? The hole? Is it the water beneath? Similarly, what is spirituality? Is it in our minds? Is it our values and beliefs? Our religiosity? Is it our very essence? These are all questions that I've asked, answered, and then realized that they were not really answered. This last realization is, for me, the most exciting. The unanswered questions cause me to continue searching.

Whenever I have thought about the well, I have wondered how it got there. Apparently, it was already there when my Mom and her sisters moved to the house shortly after my grandmother passed away. I suppose this well like others was made or dug by humans in response to a need for water. The water itself already existed underground for a very long time. Yet it was the meeting of nature and humanity that created the well. Each depended on the other to serve its purpose. The water perhaps would have never reached the surface but for human hands. Could God be like this deep running water that calls us to make a connection with the divine in order to draw life from it?

I believe that our spirituality is in fact like this relationship with the well. The source of life for the well is the water which in its relationship with humanity finds its identity and gives life to those who draw from it. In the same way, my spirituality is my well. God is my source of life, and in my daily relationship with God and all of creation, I find an identity that gives me life. This identity comes from the spirit with which we are born and which we spend our lives trying to discover. All of this takes place throughout our individual histories which include our relationships. It would therefore be impossible for me to be spiritual without taking into account my own history.

This process of drawing life from the well and the shape it takes depends upon who helped to dig the well, who deposited things into it, and who has drawn life from it. Who has been a part of my connection with God? Who has deposited or contributed? Who has drawn life from it? As I think about these and other elements of my spirituality I immediately think about fundamental values in my life. One of the strongest elements that I feel within my own spirituality is the closeness to the deceased members of my family. Much like the pebbles I used to throw into the well which caused a ripple effect, one person who has always thrown pebbles into my well has been my Mom, who told me stories about my aunts and uncles and particularly, my grandmother and Aunt Emilia. I never met my grandmother Natividad but I know her well. She and Aunt Emilia were always a part of the lives of my brothers, sisters, cousins and me. My grandmother was a hardworking woman who lived and labored for her daughters. She was the kind of woman who always had enough food to feed visitors even when there was little food to go around. Her work as a seamstress was very demanding physically and took a particular toll on her eyesight. Everything she did, all of her work and charity, was motivated by her love for her daughters. My Aunt Emilia, or Mama Melita as we called her, picked up where her mom left off and spent the whole of her life caring for her two other sisters and, eventually, her nieces and nephews. There was little of anything that my Mom did not have during her young-adult years thanks to Mama Melita. Both my grandmother Nati and Mama Melita were givers of life; it was only natural that the recipients of so much of their love would do the same for others.

How do I know someone whom I never met and am so inspired by, someone who is only a vague recollection? I suppose that it is a result of people like my Mom throwing pebbles into my well. Some of these pebbles were in the form of stories, both fictional and non-fictional. My cousin, for example, used to gather my brother and sisters and me to tell us her version of God's relationship with some of the dearly departed. According to her, every night the dead would rise and process throughout the cemetery. In their procession they lit their own way by lighting a finger as if it were a candle. According to my cousin, God's favorite deceased, which included my grandmother and other relatives, did not have to light their finger because being God's favorites, they were given their own candle. We now enjoy many laughs over this story, but for me it is also a further example of how I learned that special people like my grandmother had a special place with God, who recognized their importance. At the same time, this story helped to make death something familiar and not something to fear. I have drawn much consolation from the belief that there are special members of my family accompanying me through life and that I can call on them in moments of joy as well as in moments of uncertainty and despair.

It had been years since I had looked into the well of my spirituality, when something very unexpected occurred. One day I will always remember is the day I metaphorically fell into the well. It all happened so fast. It had been two weeks since my father first entered the hospital. The inevitable seemed near. I called upon every person and spirit I could think of for help, but there was no response. Would I finally find out the depth of the well? I was confused, insecure, and felt stripped of everything that once protected me. There was no cover on the well to save me and no rope to hold on to. I was scared. The deceased relatives and saints did not answer me. Finally, I tried to strike a deal with God, but it was no use. Had everyone abandoned me?

There was only one thing left to do. It was an idea that had been with me for as long as I can remember, but something that I had only talked about and never really done. TRUST IN

GOD. Never before had the words "your will be done" been so powerful. I remember those words circling my head and eventually coming from my heart. It was then, and only then, that I discovered just how deep the well was, and what was at the bottom. It, indeed, was water . . . not the dirty water I so often imagined, but clear running water: the Source of Life.

As I tried to surface, I realized that I was not alone. The very same people I had called upon for help had been with me all along, including my father. I watched his image fading like an image in the water after a stone had been dropped in, and I felt his last breath becoming my own. I remember leaving the hospital that cold and snowy morning. My Mom, brothers, sisters, and I would never be the same. It was in the pain of it all that I discovered the comfort of knowing "I have him forever." My father would now live forever in me. As I sat by myself the night before the burial, I thought of each member of my family and how he lived and would continue to live in all of us. It was in this new breath of air that I discovered love as I had never known it and a renewed hope that we would someday be together again.

Over the years my parents threw many pebbles into my well. As I try to discover what these are, two images emerge: love and hope. Love was always in abundance in our home, even through struggles and conflicts, and hope always burned brightly that, despite difficult times, things would someday change for the better.

As I look ahead to the future I continue to find love and hope. I discover that the love my nieces and nephews have for their grandmother motivates them to learn Spanish; their love for their grandfather is expressed in the letters, drawings and flowers they place on his grave. This new generation seems to be forming its own wells. In all of this I find hope that, while our children may possibly lose the language or customs or traditions of their past, the same spirit will remain.

5

Tía Petra's Novena

Ricardo Ramírez, C.S.B.

A Case Study—The Story of an Act of Faith

Many, many years ago, I had an experience of faith that I now remember as one of the most significant moments in my spiritual development. It is that moment in my early years that I here present as the centerpiece of this essay, written as a personal reflection on Hispanic faith. Others may find parallels in their own lives.

It was a cold night in south Texas; a "blue norther" had just come through and cleared the sky. In the cool crispness of that evening, we walked a few yards from the home of my grandparents, where my immediate family lived, to the home of Tía Petra and her family. I did not know why we were going to Tía Petra's. After supper we usually didn't have much to do with one another, especially in the winter when it was uncomfortable to leave the house. That night, everyone gathered to begin the novena to Our Lady of Guadalupe. I found out later that this was the yearly custom of the extended family. I had probably seen the *altarcito* in the corner of the main room of Tía Petra's house before but never paid too much attention to it. This time a couple of candles were lit in front of the image of Our Lady of Guadalupe, and I still remember the pictures of the four apparitions at each corner of the *altarcito*. I also remember my Tía Petra, a woman whom I had only seen in her role as tortilla-maker, clothes-washer, lunch-maker, and general *mujer de la casa*. She was a woman with a ready smile and always had a word of encouragement. That evening, she took out an old black book, with tattered, yellow-aged papers that kept falling out. She took out a rosary and began speaking to the picture at an unbelievable speed. I was entirely entranced by the whole scene; I would first look at the image with the flickering candles before it, then look at my family, concentrating on what they were saying with their eyes fixed on the image of Our Lady of Guadalupe. I don't remember just how long the scene captivated me, but I do remember very vividly what happened next.

As we were walking back to our grandparents' home that cold, dark night, I took my grandfather's hand. After walking a few paces with me, he reached down, and for no explainable reason except for his *cariño* for me, he lifted me up and sat me on his shoulder. I looked up and saw a million stars set against the black sky. It was at that moment that I sensed a special presence of the Someone who made those stars, and in child-like fashion, I surmised that all of those stars had been made for me. It was in that context of devotion to Guadalupe, family intimacy, and the sense of grandeur, that I felt that God started reaching out and initiating a life-long familiarity with me. I sincerely believe that my Christian vocation began at that very precise moment . . . and all in the milieu created by Tía Petra's novena.

Phenomenological Elements

Faith is the reaching out of God to us by means of "sacramental" mediations such as persons or groups of persons, sacred symbols, sounds, visual images, the emotions and the grandeur of creation. All of these elements were present at the time of my first act of faith. First and foremost, God spoke to me in the intimacy and security of the extended family. For me, it is an undeniable truth that a loving and personal God can only be experienced in a loving and caring environment.

At Tía Petra's, I became intrigued with the centrality of the Virgin of Guadalupe. The image was somewhat familiar; I had seen it before, since she is practically in every Mexican home.

But that particular evening, the family members focused their attention on this already familiar image.

I had no way of knowing at the time, but throughout my life the central figure of Our Lady of Guadalupe would be a permanent source of consolation, strength, and fascination. Guadalupe was to connect me with the history of the Mexican people since its *mestizo* origins in the sixteenth century. That symbol would help me to arrive at my Catholic Mexican-American identity. The image of Guadalupe was always around in my childhood, and when I had to leave my native state of Texas to go north to the seminary, I carried the image with me. Interestingly, the image was so important in my life that wherever I was assigned I made sure that the image was hung somewhere in my house or the institution of my assignment and remained there when I would leave.

As I reflect upon Tía Petra's novena, I am sure that it was there that I discovered the world of the sacred. This happened at the hearing of new and sacred utterances—my Tía Petra's rattling of prayers with the rest of the family responding. I saw objects that I had never seen before, such as the rosary and the tattered prayer book. I was further impressed by the different bodily postures and facial expressions of my family. It wasn't everyday that my family knelt together to utter sacred sounds. I was sure that something very special and extraordinary was going on, something that had to do with everything else. I couldn't explain it then, but now I know that it was a mountaintop encounter with the invisible God by way of His visible mother.

Theological Elements

The following theological themes and concepts regarding God and the act of faith were all very much present at Tía Petra's novena.

God reveals Godself. This is the basic principle of the revelation of God as described in the Dogmatic Constitution on Divine Revelation *Dei Verbum*: "It pleased God, in His goodness and wisdom, to reveal Himself and to make known the mystery of His will."[1]

The God of Jesus is the God of love, who loves from afar,

but who is also very present. In other words, our belief is in a transcendent and immanent God. In the Old Testament, God is so near that in theophanies God actually speaks directly to patriarchs, prophets, and kings. In the New Testament, the Risen Lord wants to assure his disciples of his protective nearness: "Do not fear, it is I" (Matt 14:27). In both Old and New Testaments, the ambivalence of transcendence/immanence recurs again and again. At the call of Moses, the Lord is so close, that the two talk to each other, but at the same time, the Lord maintains a distance: "Come no nearer! Remove the sandals from your feet, for the place where you stand is holy ground" (Exod 3:4-5). At the transfiguration, Jesus is transformed totally and becomes "totally-other" in an awe-inspiring gesture . . . yet there is a familiarity created and Peter is prompted to say "Lord, how good that we are here! With your permission, I will erect three booths here—one for you, one for Moses, and one for Elijah" (Matt 17:4).

The story of Our Lady of Guadalupe also reflects the transcendence/immanence of divine revelation. Our Lady speaks tenderly and lovingly to the Indian Juan Diego. They carry on some beautiful conversations together. Yet when one examines the image left of Juan's *tilma*, one notices that, while the face is that of an Indian maiden, there are other signs that indicate that she is from somewhere beyond, and not of this world. The *tilma* shows Guadalupe dressed in a mantle filled with stars; the sun is behind her back; and there is a black moon under her feet.

Another theological element that was present at Tía Petra's novena was the way in which the act of faith occurred. The beginning of the faith process is always through the mediation of someone else. We believe because others believe. Faith is therefore "caught" by way of the witnesses of those close to us. Furthermore, the act of faith involves a whole person: psychologically, emotionally, and intellectually.

Biblical References and Parallels

Reflecting upon Tía Petra's novena and my own act of faith, I see somewhat of a parallel in the Scriptures with Abraham and the promise of a progeny that would "outnumber the stars.'' Abraham and I have something in common: we both experienced the transcendent God as we beheld the cosmos.

I also see a parallel between my first act of faith and Moses and the burning bush. My ''burning bush'' was the scene of my extended family gathered around the candle-lit image of the Virgin of Guadalupe. Like Moses, I was surprised by what was happening, and at the same time, captivated. The God of Moses was the God of Tía Petra.

If it is true—and I really believe this—that my vocation to the Christian life and to the priesthood came that night, then the experience has parallels in the *anawim*, the little people in the history of salvation. God's revelation and purpose so often happen in the Scriptures through the young, humble, and poor, such as David, Saul, Isaiah, Elizabeth, Joseph, Simeon, and Anna, to name but a few. I am now the Bishop of Las Cruces, then I was a three- or four-year-old child of a migrant family.

I am sure that there have been times in my life that I had fearful images of God, of someone who judges severely, but I have never failed to believe that the God who is and will be forever is a loving God, as described in John 3:16: ''God so loved the world, that he sent his only Son.''

The Scriptures often relate the mystery of vocation both in the Old and the New Testaments. We don't know exactly why God chose the Jews, nor why God chose Abraham, Moses, or Jacob. At the moment of initial vocation, there is no reason why the prophets were chosen, for some admitted their ignorance and their unworthiness. The same thing happened in the New Testament with Peter who stumbles around, with Philip who questions everything, and with Thomas who doubts it all. Paul admittedly acknowledges his own wrestling with his call, since he did not witness the resurrection. Those of us who have been called to priesthood often question, ''Why me?'' and in my case, ''Why did God choose me; there are so many others with far greater intellectual, spiritual, and human capacities?'' That is the mystery of vocation.

In the Scriptures, particularly in Luke and John, Mary has a unique place in the history of salvation. Her presence in the Scriptures never takes away from her Son, Jesus Christ. He is always the star, or the sun, and she the moon, reflecting only the light that she receives from her Son. Perhaps my first act of faith is parallel to the placing of the mother of Jesus in John's Gospel at the beginning of his earthly mission at the wedding feast of Cana. She later appears in John only at the end of the Gospel, at the foot of the cross. The mother of Jesus in John seems to provide the framework for the entire Gospel. While she is not mentioned in the many chapters in between, by appearing at the beginning and at the end, Mary seems to be always present, but in the background. In my own spiritual journey, the mother of Jesus has always been there, caring, nurturing, understanding, and often simply listening.

The Reality and Function of Hispanic Popular Catholicism

Hispanic popular Catholicism, even in these post-Vatican II times, with the emphasis on the official prayer of the Church in the liturgy, still enjoys a strong and active presence. It affects people in deep and indelible ways, as is true in my own life. The impact of Hispanic popular Catholicism does not go away, even after a sophisticated, European-centered theological education, as is the case with all North American priests.

I am convinced that popular Catholicism connects us with our ancestors. Our acts of faith are not historically disconnected, but part of a continuous flow of faith that reaches back hundreds of years. This, of course, is part of our Judeo-Christian heritage, for we firmly believe in the same God of Abraham, Moses, Jacob, Mary, Joseph, and Jesus. But our faith is also the faith of Juan Diego, Santa Rosa de Lima, San Martín de Porres, Oscar Arnulfo Romero and Tía Petra. It is the faith of the Spanish missionaries, of the converted Indians of Mexico, of the *mestizo* people of the sixteenth century, of the *insurgentes* of the war for independence of 1810, of struggling peasants under Porfirio Díaz, of the revolutionaries of 1910, and of the Cristeros of the 1920s. To remember the faith of ancestors is to remember the gift of faith and the burden that is connected with it, that is, the responsibility to keep the faith alive and to pass it on to the succeeding generation. My faith, then, has significance, not only for myself and for my salvation, but for the salvation of those whom I do not know because they are not yet born, but whom I will know in the new heavens and in the new earth.

Hispanic popular Catholicism is also a conveyor of faith and values. It has a formative influence on people. It influences a person's prioritization of his or her life. It is a subtle yet real influence on one's societal relationships. It speaks of an invisible world of fairness, equality, respect, dignity, and happiness where things are right. The symbolic world of popular Catholicism is a constant reminder that wrongs will be righted, that justice will prevail, and that God will "remember."

Conclusion

It is my hope that the preceding personal reflections will assist the reader in ascertaining what is unique about Hispanic spirituality. The subject is both complex and intriguing. Other Christian cultural groups might see parallels to what we describe as "Hispanic." Perhaps it is a matter of focus and emphasis that the Hispanics place on specific aspects of faith or devotion. For most Hispanic Catholics the way of faith and the processes of conversion take place in the context of popular Catholicism. It is through popular Catholicism that the world of the sacred is entered and experienced. The richness of that gift is what Hispanics bring to the liturgy, the official prayer of the Church. We cannot come empty handed to the altar of God and to the house of the family of God when we come for worship. This builds upon what we learn at home, in the family, from the close and intimate people in our lives. It begins in all of us when we are infants and is nurtured throughout our lives as we grow in stature, wisdom, and grace.

The phenomenon of Hispanic popular Catholicism is real and undeniably powerful. I owe Tía Petra my profound gratitude for placing me on the threshold of faith and for giving me the trajectory of my vocation.

NOTE

1. Ricardo Ramírez, C.S.B., "Hispanic Spirituality," *Social Thought* (Summer, 1985) 6-15.

6

Memories of My Hispanic Adolescence

María Teresa Gastón Witchger

Before I became a mother, I used to tell people, "I wish kids were born as teenagers." Most people looked at me like I was crazy. They were obviously influenced by all the bad press young people receive. Having thrived through my own youth and having worked with teens for over ten years, I think that adolescence represents an exciting time of growth and becoming.

Adolescence can be defined as "a chronological period beginning with the physical and emotional processes leading to sexual and psychosocial maturity and ending at an ill-defined time when the individual achieves independence and social productivity. The period is associated with rapid physical, psychological and social changes."[1] Defined this way, my adolescence lasted about ten years: from the onset of puberty at twelve until I was twenty-three, when I graduated from college, left home, and took a job in another city. For other Hispanic youth who form their own families and work to support themselves at a much earlier age, adolescence may last as little as four or five years.

Adolescence is a time to begin confronting questions such as "Who am I?" "Where do I belong?" "What am I going to do with my life?" and "With whom am I going to share my life?" These questions of identity, intimacy and commitment motivate the adolescent to relate to God in a new way.

39

In this article I would like to trace how my spirituality as a Cuban-American adolescent developed in three ways, as: Christ-centered, relational and justice-oriented. I will also try to focus on how my Cubanness influenced my developing spirituality.

"La Virgen y los santos" (the Virgin and the saints) and getting to heaven played an important role in my parents' spirituality. Mine grew much more Christ-centered. I was influenced by my sister's conversion to fundamentalism and by the Church's post-conciliar emphasis on Jesus, Scripture, laity in mission, and the kingdom now. As I look back, this is how I see my faith development.

My parents came to this country from Cuba when I was three years old. When I was six we moved from Miami to Milwaukee and later to New Berlin, a suburb, where I grew up and attended public schools through the eighth grade. Isolated from our large extended family and Cuban community, my parents chose to assimilate in American life as much as they could. This was not difficult as my parents both spoke English and we are light-skinned.

Mom maintained some sense of culture with Cuban food, music and correspondence with relatives. She was freer about speaking the language and talking about Cuba. She would light a *velita* in front of our statue of *La Virgen de la Caridad* on special feast days of remembering, and make an effort to celebrate our saints' days.

Dad, on the other hand, was self-conscious of his accent and worked hard to improve his English to avoid discrimination at work. He repressed a lot of pain associated with his leaving Cuba. It was almost as though he made the decision never to look back. He suggested once that I tell people we were French and recommended that I take French over Spanish in school.

I did not follow this advice. I enjoyed telling people I was Cuban, even though I spoke halting Spanish and knew virtually no Cuban history, geography, or literature. I remember feeling deprived, sad and even angry at times that I had no memories of my own of Cuba and that I had missed out on our life there. I don't remember ever talking to my parents or anyone about this as an adolescent.

In Cuba being Catholic was very much a part of our culture and family identity. Two of my older sisters became nuns soon after leaving Cuba. When we finally settled in suburban Milwaukee, we actively participated in an all English speaking parish which was a warm and alive community with intelligent and inspiring leadership.

It came as a great shock to the family when my sister Marge became a fundamentalist "Bible Christian" at age nineteen and "left the Church." My parents were very hurt and confused by her condemnation of the Church. They forbade her from talking to me about religion, but of course we did anyway. The Scripture passages she gave me to read and our prayer together helped me relate to Jesus more personally and gave me growing confidence as a Christian, but I was confused about her emphasis on the end times, the devil, and the anti-Christ. It served to arouse questions about Christianity, faith, the history of the Church and the sacraments, Jesus and his teachings.

Gratefully, my parish was a good place to turn with my questions. There I found many opportunities to share with people who welcomed my search and led me in the direction of the best of Catholic theology. I also became active in youth retreats through my school and parish. This is when the relational dimension of my spirituality began to grow. In relationships with friends, teachers, priests and other adults, I experienced how wonderful it is to share deeply, to be honest and vulnerable, to be accepted and loved. On retreat I met Catholics who freely witnessed to their faith in Christ, but who also drew implications for life that seemed much more holistic to me. Sexuality and relationships were not something evil to be avoided, but a gift and responsibility to be enjoyed and handled maturely, and a place where one encounters God! The community prayer and sharing experiences of the retreats helped me begin to work out some of the confusion caused by Marge's influence. I slowly realized that I wanted to "stay Catholic" and to grow in my relationship with Christ in the community of the Church. I had not yet dealt with my cultural identity.

During these years I had to wear a brace from neck to hips twenty-three hours a day to correct a curvature in my spine. I hated it in many ways, but it was a good counselor. It helped me grow in self-knowledge and self-acceptance as well as empathy and concern for people who suffered in different ways. I began to reach out to the loners at school and found myself becoming interested in books about the Jewish and Black experience.

In college relationships continued to broaden and deepen my spirituality. People I met in groups such as Bread for the World and The Catholic Worker movement nurtured a growing dimension of spirituality linked with work for justice—a commitment to what I was coming to understand as Jesus' mission of bringing about the reign of God.

I was happy to learn I had enough Cubanness in me to relate to people from different countries in the International Student Association and other Hispanics in the *Club Latino Estudiantil.* Juan Alvarez, an articulate and formerly militant Chicano, became a good friend. He introduced me to the Chicano struggle for identity and freedom. My family's experience of exile and diaspora after leaving Cuba was so different from the oppression Mexican Americans experienced as they lost their language, culture, and autonomy in their own land.

Through campus ministry, I became involved with the broader Milwaukee Hispanic community for the first time. I volunteered in a bilingual elementary school. Eventually I accepted a job teaching English at the Spanish Center at night. I was surprised how comfortably I related to these children and adults from Puerto Rico and Mexico and other countries. They welcomed me into their homes. I felt privileged and enriched by their stories, food, and friendship. They helped me lose my fear and self-consciousness of speaking Spanish. I was so grateful for this new "Hispanic" me they nurtured! My parents were not thrilled with my growing involvement on the southside of the city. When I asked to bring home three Mexican students from my English class for Thanksgiving dinner, I remember my father telling me, "Tewe, that's your mission, don't make it mine." Mom would say to me, "Charity begins at home!"

I often prayed that God would show me what I was supposed to do with my life. I had valuable experience in youth ministry. I was deeply interested in theology and ministry, political and social science and action. I was not attracted to religious life and I was in no hurry to get married. How would I give myself as a lay woman in the Church?

It was the experience of participating in the process of the *II Encuentro Nacional Hispano de Pastoral* that gave me a sense of vocation that helped me to integrate my identity as a Christian and as a Hispanic. I learned about Freire's liberating adult education, about small Christian communities, about cultural pluralism and international human rights. To have Church, from the grass-roots of Hispanic communities all over the United States reflecting and making connections between these themes seemed almost too good to be true. This is the kind of Church I wanted to be part of.

The incredible diversity of the North American Hispanic Catholic community was overwhelming. The experience of fitting in, of belonging, of being called forth as a young Hispanic woman was wonderfully encouraging. The challenge to work together as *Pueblo de Dios en Marcha* was exciting. I discovered that my gifts and experience in youth ministry met a real need in the Hispanic Catholic community and to this I dedicated myself.

Even though I was raised with a weak sense of my Cuban identity, I believe my Cubanness played an important role in my developing spirituality as an adolescent. Perhaps it was my unspoken sense of loss, my desire to find a missing part of me, that made me want to form relationships with people of different cultures. My ability to speak even hesitant Spanish made it possible for me to enter the world of Hispanics with backgrounds very different from mine and there to encounter God. My family history contributed to my interest in politics and world events. The more I learned about the inequalities and maldistribution of wealth and power, the more I developed a spirituality that seeks justice.

My spirituality today is still relational and justice-oriented, grounded in the person and mission of Jesus. As an adolescent it was more future-commitment-oriented. Now I struggle to be faithful as a wife and mother in living out my commitments made to Christ and to the *pueblo* in the migrant farmworker community where we live.

I would like to close by recalling the challenge offered to us by the national Hispanic Pastoral Plan to form healing, nurturing faith communities where adolescents can encounter and respond to Jesus' loving invitation to ''come, follow me.'' For an Hispanic young person living in two cultures the process of achieving secure identity, healthy intimacy and fruitful commitment is complicated by competing standards and conflicting role expectations. What parents demand is different from what peers want and conflicts with what school and society expect.

Can the Church be a place where Hispanic youth can safely sort out these role conflicts with the aid of supportive adults and peers? Can our parishes be a place where Hispanic adolescents can discover an identity as Christians without negating or suppressing their cultural uniqueness? Can a Christian community offer Hispanic youth an opportunity to experience trusting, honest relationships and develop their capacity for intimacy? Can small Christian communities empower Hispanic youth to discover their own gifts and the needs in the world around them and begin to see how they might serve meaningfully in their adult lives? These are some of the questions that come to mind as I reflect on my own developing spirituality as an adolescent and compare it with the needs of Hispanic youth I know today.

NOTE

1. Armand Nicoli, ed., *Harvard Guide to Modern Psychiatry* (Cambridge: Belknap Press, 1978) 519.

7

The Spirituality of One Hispanic Marriage

Olga Villa Parra

The word "spiritual" comes from the Latin word *spiritualis* that can mean "of breathing, of wind, of relating to, consisting of, or affecting the spirit." Another definition is "related or joined in spirit." It is around this definition that my husband Ricardo and I have lived and built our marriage.

This contribution is written from a very personal and intimate perspective. To share one's spirituality, one must be intimate; to be intimate is to experience life and feel vulnerable. This seems quite natural within the context of my Hispanic heritage as well as my life with Ricardo. For me spirituality is an ongoing process which unfolds every day with and through the grace of God. Spirituality is the essence of our marriage, love and life struggles. We identify and are nurtured and have a fidelity to this essence. Ricardo and I encounter joy in our marriage as well as with our *pueblo* and the communities with whom we share life.

El Nacimiento

Walking through the woods, playing with other children, and listening for mother calling are some of my earliest memories as a young child. I didn't understand at the time, but the seeds of love for community, family, and marriage values were being planted then. My mother was the promoter and architect of our faith and Hispanic world. My father was a typical papa:

a strong, faithful husband who worked hard to sustain his family. Our family represented the struggling migrant family that had settled in an upstream northern state—large, poor and happy. We had our struggles, yet found happiness in our faith and family.

My parents were persistent in what they understood as essential to the spiritual life: attending Mass, involvement with the parish outreach programs, and our attendance at Sunday catechism classes. Among my mother's daily litanies were her *dichos*: "Sin la Fe, no hay vida" ("Without faith there is no life"), "Dios primero" ("God first"), "Tu eres hija de Dios" ("You are God's daughter"), or her favorite saying to express displeasure: "Te vas, pero sin mi bendición" ("Go ahead, but without my blessing"). It was against this backdrop that I ventured out into the world full of faith, energy, and wonderment.

Another important foundation was the faith community in which our family participated. Our family was part of a new church mission which eventually became a parish at the outskirts of a small city. Our priests were Franciscans who had been exiled from China during the revolution. They were wise, older, and loving individuals. They inculcated in us the values of prayer in work and daily life. Prayer was an action woven into our daily lives, so our whole life took on a spiritual dimension.

El Encuentro

I remember the exact moment I decided to marry Ricardo Parra. We were someplace having a very intellectual conversation. At this time I can't even remember where we were, or what the discussion was about. All of a sudden, Ricardo interrupted our conversation with a very terse statement. "If you [Olga] want to be around me, you have to understand what I believe in and what I stand for." I was stunned; it had absolutely nothing to do with our conversation. Yet, I knew intuitively that something profound was about to happen in my life. So being the person that I am and needing more time to digest the statement, I pretended that I did not understand. I asked him to explain. The result was a greater understanding of Ricardo's spirituality, and the start of our lives together.

Our beginnings were very humble. We had few material possessions, but a wealth of friends, and enough vision and mission for two lifetimes. So began our not so common journey into a relationship and marriage, and the search for direction and answers to our common concerns. This journey began with a relationship based on social justice and a commitment to the Hispanic community. One thing that contributed greatly to our journey was that both of us came from large families that had suffered economically and socially in our *barrios*. We were also children of the 60s and early on had been sensitized to the larger societal questions of social change and equality.

Un Camino Espiritual

With this common history we embarked upon our joint quest. I have always operated from a profound, intuitive spirituality that springs from the popular faith of people and communities. It is a spirituality that is most stimulated by relationships with nature and humanity. Ricardo's challenge to me—stemming from that eventful day when he called me to understand and believe what he stood for—is to be clear about what I believe and stand for. I was challenged to articulate my intuitive spirituality and what I understood to be its meaning.

In 1979, Ricardo and I were married. What an event, equal from our perspective only to a royal wedding. We wrote our vows, married in the custom of the Aztec wedding of our ancestors, in the context of an updated Roman Catholic tradition, followed by one great, giant fiesta. Our wedding costs were practically non-existent, because family, friends, and community pitched in to make it happen. Our wedding day was another milestone on our spiritual journey. We worked with a friend to develop the wedding vows and to practice them for the ceremony. We selected our friends who would participate in the wedding ceremony as if we were constructing spiritual pillars to help and protect us along our marriage journey. I knew that this event would have a profound impact on all who attended. After the wedding Ricardo and I sensed that we truly had been bonded together in service to the holy mission of life.

El Desafio

Being related to Ricardo was a spiritual journey in itself. We faced the basic challenge of how to live a marriage of fidelity and responsibility. We were assuming a faithful union and also the responsibilities that come from accepting a partner and from family responsibilities. We were cautious of being cast into traditional Hispanic roles of husband and wife, and we did not want to lose our individual identities or stop growing as human beings. We were adults living in a new world, with new friends and even a new position in the family structure.

Still the values of our parents and families persisted and were fundamental for our marriage and our interaction with others. We began to share our dreams. We built our home and as we grappled with our new roles as husband and wife, our love has grown strong. Yet the journey into marriage presented challenging opportunities that called us to realign our thinking and to change. One such challenge for Ricardo and me was the issue of our names. I could not change my name, Olga Villa. *Ademas Olga Villa es el nombre de mi familia.* Eventually, my name became Olga Villa Parra. Ricardo would kid me that the only time I would use "Parra" was when we went to visit his family, which was true. On the other hand, he told me the day of our wedding that his real name was Ramon Ricardo Parra. Yet, he had always gone by Richard Parra. These moments may seem insignificant, yet they can become occasions of considerable consternation.

I don't believe any marriage is problem-free. Imperfect understanding, incomplete acceptance, and half-hearted affirmation are all part of our day by day struggles for a meaningful life together. In a sense, spiritual growth is a process of ongoing problem solving, for we are not born with the gift of intimacy. We must grow into mutual intimacy gradually and, at times, painfully. Human intimacy is a powerful experience, and it takes extraordinary effort to be good communicators. The longer we have been married, the more important communication has become. We have continued to grow as individuals and together in mutual spirituality. We were both fertile with love, wanting to give life to others. We were not blessed with children. Yet, our relationship blossomed as we built our lives together and shared our home with our families and the others who came into our lives. "Nuestra casa es su casa" took on a new meaning. We have had students and people from many walks of life and various countries of the world live with us in our home. We tried to create a family environment in which they became part of our family and our home was truly their home. This experience has been a blessing to us and has enriched our lives. We understand our marriage as a gift of friendship and intimacy. We will continue to share and build our unique Hispanic spirituality on "El amor de nuestras familias y comunidad es el amor que cumple" ("The love of our families and community is the love that fulfills").

Philip Sherrard states:

> The final enfolding of mutual love, that alone in which the full sacramental union between man and woman is achieved, is not an acquisition but a benediction. It is conferred by the Creator on two creatures, man and woman, who have run the course of their love through whatever it may have led them and have entered, transfigured at last, the holy ground of their being.[1]

Our lives have not yet run their course, but the journey has transfigured us . . . a journey that is certainly a benediction for us and for those whom we serve.

NOTE

1. Philip Sherrard. *Christianity and Eros: Essays on the Theme of Sexual Love* (London: SPCK, 1976) 93.

8

The Spirituality of a Hispanic Priest

Juan Sosa

She rang the bell at the rectory and I opened the door. I was on duty that bright morning in early February. She needed to see a priest and I invited her into my office; indeed, her mannerisms indicated the need to talk, and so she did: "Father, I was born in Peru and was raised in a good school, but my parents only baptized me. I received no other religious instruction. Now I want to receive First Communion and confirmation."

I was amazed. Do adults actually ring the door of our rectories to seek the sacraments? Most of the time I seem to be finding ways to motivate them to encounter Jesus sacramentally. This was different; she truly wants to receive the Lord! I grew more delighted by the minute, but her frankness prompted me to ask the basic question: "Why now? What pushed you to do this?" Her answer came out quickly in the form of a story.

"You see, Father, I am married. My husband is also Catholic, though he hardly ever goes to church. We have a son who is now four years old and who attends a Lutheran pre-school down the street where they taught him how to pray. Every night my husband and I spend some time with my son before he goes to sleep. We watch him pray before he gets into bed, and we pray with him." She continued, "At least I make believe I am praying, since I know not how to pray. I always stay quiet and watch him say his prayers . . . except for this one night.'' She stopped to catch her breath while I listened attentively.

"He caught me not praying, not moving my lips, simply sitting there and he asked me point blank: 'Mummy, why don't you pray with me?' At first I did not know what to say, but I told him the truth. 'Mummy does not pray because she never had the opportunity to learn her prayers as you do now.'

"And then he blurted it out: 'Don't worry mummy, I WILL TEACH YOU,' he said. 'I WILL TEACH YOU.' You see, Father, a four-year-old boy, my son, willing to teach me . . . it was as if God were talking directly to me through him . . . and now I am here. . . .''

*   *   *   *   *

At times we place ourselves on pedestals and seek power in strange ways: at work, in the church, through our parish. The closer we are to the top, the better we think we will feel. But where is our God? At the top, on the bottom, or by the side? We fail to recognize God's voice, touch, and love. We grow too busy to believe in the divine Epiphany among us. Here was our God, speaking through a child, who reached out almost beyond human imagination to rescue his parents from their indifference.

This story took place during my first year as a priest. Twenty years later, I remember it as vividly as the day it happened. It taught me many things, but in particular, a way to the spiritual life and how to encounter God, whose infinite love cannot be measured and whose ways among us cannot be predicted. My reflections on this experience have had a great impact in my life. How often I have asked myself, "Did I perceive that God called me to ministry in my interaction with this Peruvian lady, whose self-sufficient life had been shattered to pieces by the soothing intervention of her child?'' As I become more aware that this story is only one among many in my ministry, I am beginning to recognize similarities between the spiritual journey of Hispanic Catholics and my own spiritual journey as a human being and as a priest.

Well-educated or not, middle-class Latin Americans or Mexican migrants, Hispanics share a spiritual journey filled with ambiguity, paradox, and joy. First, there is a sense of pilgrimage that gives meaning in the midst of family and social crises. Second, there is a great need to experience family support and warmth. Third, there is the search for a wider community (church) that may complement the absence of an extended family unit. Finally, there is an openness to the gentle touch of a God who leads us through our insecurity into the healing peace of the divine embrace. In our powerlessness, God becomes real and becomes a true companion in our pilgrimage.

The priest in me must walk with other Hispanics down this path!

A Pilgrim

As I journey in pilgrimage, I wonder at the world around me, sometimes afraid of its rapid changes. At other times, I am aware of my mission through which I can reach "sanctity": a wholeness of mind and heart with God at the center of my pilgrimage. Fear disappears before me as I journey in faith.

Am I alone? Undoubtedly not, though at times I feel lonely. I rejoice with the Lord for not allowing me to settle down so much that I can become stale and comfortable with myself and my ministry. Like Paul in his missionary travels, I, at times, feel the need to reach out to those whom I have served in the past. Telephone calls may have substituted for writing, but the experience is the same: to remember by making present among us God's loving presence through our stories. And as I come to know new people, I can readily recognize the voice, the hands, the love of the Lord in them. I know I am not called to the stability of this life, but to a different and invigorating experience that will never end.

A Family Member

I used to think that a priest must leave his family behind once he embraced the ministry fully. True and false. One can never leave behind those roots where the experience of ministry began. What could I be without my family? As we gather to share experiences during the holidays, a sense of tradition arises among us which is difficult to explain.

I cannot impose myself on others at these family gatherings. "My cousin, the priest," at times, may become the focus of our conversations. Instead, I wish it was Jesus within them who calls them to change, to grow, and to serve others. I am not the only one called to serve. All of the baptized are. How much we could be doing as a family if we all took this baptismal calling seriously.

Let those among us who are estranged find a way to reconcile themselves. Why fight over personal opinions or preferences? In the Lord we are all equal. God has no favorites. In Jesus we have all become one. Through Jesus we can all experience happiness and peace.

A Servant of the Church

I have loved this title ever since I first heard it during Scripture classes. It comes from the Songs of Isaiah announcing the experiences of God's preferred Servant, and it brings to our Good Friday services a dramatic presence and pathos:

> See, my servant shall prosper . . . it was our infirmities that he bore, our sufferings that he endured. . . . Like a lamb led to slaughter . . . he was silent and opened not his mouth. . . . He shall take away the sins of many. . . .
>
> (Isa 52:13; 53:4, 7, 12)

What does it mean for me?

A priest is a servant when he orients his life to others, when their needs become important to him, when he feels free to serve them because he knows how to deal with his own needs, when he takes care of himself so that he can take care of others better, when he is willing to pass through death and resurrection as part of his journey of life and, thus, dares to live the Paschal Mystery to the fullest.

In and through the Church I live as a servant, especially when I feel the burden of my ministry. The Church with its foibles and its gifts—composed of human beings called to holi-

ness, who are prophetic and loving, at times cautious and in-
quisitive of others, the Church as the sacrament of Christ in
the world—this is the larger community for me. The experience
of people assembling to pray and to transform into action the
music they sing by truly caring for their neighbors, this is the
Church, the body of Christ, the People of God, the Church
of 1492 or 1992, our Church. How can anyone substitute any
other groups or objects for it? I have difficulty understanding
others' anger or frustration with the larger community. Let
them come back to see our Church blossom in time and space,
always reaching out to reveal Emmanuel.

Open to God

I have heard this phrase so many times that it sometimes
becomes a cliché: "open to God," as distinct from closed or
apathetic or indifferent, rigid or inflexible or clerical.

For me the meaning of this phrase is embodied in a very
basic attitude in which I try to grow. "Open to God" means
not being judgmental or critical; being always ready to grow
and willing to admit to my mistakes; never being fully graduated from my life or Church, but always willing to learn; and,
above all, being able to recognize our Lord in the joys and pains
of others, and my own human experience. Being open to God
calls me not only to forgive others, but also to forgive myself
for simply being on the journey and, at times, being unwill-
ing to surrender to God's will.

The spirituality of this presbyter of Cuban ancestry, who
has grown up in the United States and has been shaped by
a Church in transition, is a patchwork spirituality, composed
of many elements. It is a spirituality that discovers the closeness of God through my need to be close to people and to find
in them the living presence of a loving parent. It is an awareness that God, in divine self-awareness, plays tricks on us
while, at the same time, guiding us through this life until we
enter into the divine embrace in the next life. It is a spirituality
of paradox and ambiguity: caught by the child-like demands
of the elderly and the gentle persistence of the young; sharing the gospel with the rich and the poor without alienating

either, while asking both to live it completely; experiencing power and strength in neither title nor fame, but in the powerlessness of life and the victory of the cross. It is a spirituality that calls me, as a priest, to continue to tell stories.

9

My Spiritual Journey

Confesor De Jesús

Introduction

Life is a constant search to find meaning. Often we feel frustrated, disoriented, or lost in this search. We are in constant search for a better life, a better education, a more comfortable house, a nicer car and a better job. Yet all of these things do not make us feel that we have found the answer to our questions. There is something missing that is needed in order to feel happiness and hope in our lives. There are times that we do not have answers to our questions. We do not have peace in our hearts and we do not realize what is going on with our lives. These are very dangerous moments in which we could move in the wrong direction, make incorrect decisions, or do nothing. These are the times when we need someone to guide us. These are the times when we find ourselves trying to understand the real meaning of our lives.

It is my intention to share several episodes of my life that contributed to my formation as a human being, as well as a spiritual man. The decisions that I made were not always the right ones, but through the course of life those decisions helped me to understand myself and realize what was missing in my life.

My Grandfather's Death

I was very close to my grandfather. When he died, I was

only eleven years old. I remember the night before he died, I was alone in my room, praying to God to heal my grandfather. The following day, about 6:00 a.m., my sister woke me up and gave me the painful news. Our grandpa just passed away. This was very difficult to accept. Why did God not answer my prayer? I was upset, disappointed, and very confused. I tried to look for an explanation for his death. I could not find one that made me feel comfortable. Since that moment my relation with God started to break down. I started having doubts about God. Later, when I was seventeen years old, I made the decision that God did not exist, that it was just a story. My life changed drastically. From a very reserved young man, I developed into a very self-reliant individual.

As a university student I openly professed that God was just a myth. I became involved with political groups, became physically violent, and made myself the center of my life. I did not share these thoughts and feelings with my family. I stopped attending church. I made new friends who held to the same political and religious ideology. Also, I started to drink and later to experiment with drugs. I made the decision that through the application of logic, I could find answers to all my questions. In other words, I was in total control of my life.

My First Marriage

This was more a reaction than an action. I was living with my father, and he told me that he was planning to remarry. It did not matter that I agreed with his decision. I thought that it was time for me to get married too. I was twenty-five when I married and remained married for three years. This was one of the most difficult experiences in my life, but at the same time it was also a great challenge to what I considered my rational way of living. I tried to resolve my marriage problems using logic. Logic had always worked for me in the past and marriage would not be the exception to this rule. The more I tried, the more confused I became. My first reaction was to handle it in a rough way. I am the man and everything will be done my way. It did not work. I started to drink every day, to use drugs more frequently and to spend seven days a week in my office. It did not work.

One night I was in a bar drinking and one of the guys said to me, "Confesor, this is not the place for you. . . . Stop drinking and rearrange your life . . . do not destroy your life . . . you have a good job . . . you are a professional . . . you have values." I looked at him and said, "You are right." I paid the bill and went to my father's house. That night I could not sleep; my problems, my questions were very present in me. About 3:00 in the morning, very deep in my heart, without words, I said to God, "I have been saying that you are not for real, but if you exist, please let me know what to do." I was expecting a light to come through my window, or a cross, or Jesus' face to appear on the wall of my bedroom. Nothing happened the way I was expecting. One more time I was trying through logic to anticipate God's reaction. In the morning when I was eating breakfast, my grandmother came from her room to talk to me. She used to go to church every day, but since her leg was amputated, she had to depend on us to get her to church. She was the only one in the family who was very religious—the rest of the family only attended Mass on special occasions. She said to me, "I know that you don't like people to be involved in your personal life, but this is what you have to do—get a divorce." She turned her wheelchair around and went back to her room. The only thing I said was "Okay, Grandma," and left for the office. As I sat in my office, it suddenly occurred to me, "You asked God for an answer, God gave it to you through your grandma." I looked to God for help, and God helped through the only person who really knew him, my grandma. He showed me that he was not a magician, and that he need not paint a cross in my room. He showed me through my grandmother's love, where he really wants to be in my life. He wants to be in my heart and be the center of my life. This changed my life completely. I started turning to God and attending church more frequently. I realized that with God there is always hope, compassion, and understanding.

A True Encounter

In 1975 I became a good friend of the parish priest. Every time that we had an opportunity, we talked and shared personal experiences. We looked in the church records to find out who my godparents were for baptism and confirmation, because I did not know them. He also encouraged me to make my First Communion and to participate in a *Cursillo de Cristiandad.*

I went to the *cursillo.* The first two days I was very uncomfortable and felt like I was in the wrong place. On the third day I started to realize the need for a life transformation. I met Jesus and asked him to be my friend. This was a true encounter with the Lord. I made the decision to change my life, and I did so for a few months. As time passed, however, I started to skip the *cursillo* weekly meeting, making poor excuses for my absence. When any problem arose in my life, I blamed Jesus. Under the influence of alcohol, I questioned why I met him. Every time I wanted to do something for personal pleasure, there was Jesus, telling me that it was wrong. I asked him to leave me alone and to stay away from me. But the seed of his love was already in my heart. I invited him to be my best friend and he accepted.

One day a friend invited me to go to the last night (Sunday) of a men's *cursillo.* I had nothing to do and I accepted his invitation. At the end of the *cursillo* I saw a good friend that I had not seen for more than five years. This friend and I were together from grammar school all the way through the university. He said to me, "Please, Confesor, do not leave, I want to talk with you." When he returned, he said, "After the second day of the *cursillo,* I wanted to leave, but I stayed because of you. I said to myself, if Confesor, who had been a worse person than I was, had made the *cursillo,* then I could do it too." Without realizing it, the Lord used me to touch my friend. This was a clear message that Jesus was a true friend.

Deacon Ordination

I was ordained a deacon in May 1986. The months of March, April, and May of that year were a time of real struggle in my life. I had been married (second time) for more than twelve years. We had four children (one boy and three girls), and we were very involved in the church as a family and as a couple. In November 1985 we participated in a married couples retreat. We were invited to give a talk in that retreat. It was a wonderful and beautiful opportunity to work together, to share our lives with others, and to bring hope to those couples in need. We were really doing God's work. That day, when we returned from the retreat, we picked up the children and we went home. We wanted to take with us some gifts that we had bought for a birthday party that night.

When we went inside the house we did not find the presents, and we realized that someone had broken into the house. They took the presents, VCR, radio, and some cash. Our first reaction was one of disappointment, but immediately we gave thanks to God because nothing happened to us. I did not realize that this incident was just a little rock in my life. Our lives started changing very drastically. We stopped praying together, we stopped going to church together, we started to argue more frequently and very strongly; the flame of love started to die. Our communication became more a formality than a desire. Our attitude and behavior was affecting the children. Our relationship was practically over.

I had to make a decision. My marriage was over; what am I going to do about the diaconate? I was only two weeks from the ordination, and I was fighting with my feelings, commitment and my spiritual life. I made the decision not go to ahead with the diaconate program. I wouldn't participate in any more church activities. In other words, I was going to quit—but I have never been a quitter. I have had a constant fight with Jesus. I told him that I was not strong enough to overcome this problem. I shared my thoughts and feelings with my spiritual director, a deacon in my parish. The week before my ordination, we talked together and he cried with me. He made my suffering and pain his suffering and pain. But he said, ''Go ahead with the ordination because God is calling you. Now, we do not understand what is happening to you, but we need to trust God and allow him to guide your life.'' This was a real struggle, but I put my confidence, my heart, and my problems in the hand of the Lord. I was ordained on Pentecost Day, the feast that celebrates the beginning of the Church and the beginning of a new man.

My marriage ended in divorce: my son is living with me and I am in touch with my daughters. I learned to put my life totally in Jesus' hands. This experience, in turn, has allowed me to help other brothers and sisters in the same situation. I do not know exactly what God's plan is for me, but I know it is a good one.

Spiritual Growth

In my parish I am a member of the charismatic group team. During the fall of 1990 the team asked me to be a candidate for the steering committee of the Hispanic Catholic Charismatic Renewal Group in Chicago. I was very pleased and affirmed by the confidence the team has in me as a committed servant of God. The committee is responsible for coordinating all the charismatic activities in the archdiocese of Chicago. Also, this group provides the guidelines for all the prayer groups affiliated with them. My name was presented to the election committee for consideration and the interview process. This committee called several men and women for interviews, but did not call me. When our prayer group questioned them regarding my candidacy, they indicated that due to my divorced status I did not qualify according to them for the steering committee. This was a great blow to my spiritual life. On one hand the Church did not prevent me from becoming a deacon; on the other hand, the same Church made judgments about my ministerial ability based on my marital status. I was disqualified without any explanation or consideration as a group member, a deacon or as a Christian.

My parish team fought this decision, and the steering committee allowed me to become a candidate. Many of the prayer groups in the archdiocese knew the committee's opposition to my candidacy. The day of the candidate presentation, the committee made clear their feelings and position regarding my candidacy. Over and over during the course of that morning, they made reference to my marital status and how they could not explain or justify a leader who was divorced. I was very hurt. I never expected that this group would reject or oppose my desire to be more committed in the Church. I felt that they crucified me without giving me an opportunity to be heard or without taking the time to understand my position. I was called and given three minutes in which to explain why I wanted to be a candidate. This was a very painful and difficult situation for me. Some of my thoughts were to play the same game that they were playing. I said to myself, I know their life, I know what is happening in their family. I know I am as qualified as they are theologically, spiritually, and academically. But I said, "Jesus, I want to do your will, please help me." Immediately a Bible passage came to my mind from the Book of Sirach. "My son, when you come to serve the Lord, prepare yourself for trials. . . ." (2:1-6). I read the verses and went back to my seat. I was not elected, but my spiritual life grew more with my sincere commitment to allow Jesus to guide my life.

Conclusion

Through these five specific episodes and others in my life, I have discovered how much the Lord really loves me. There was not a moment that I was alone, even though I felt that way. There was not a single moment that the Lord stopped caring for me. I know there will come more moments in my life that will be painful. I am not looking for them, but if I need to suffer it is better when I am doing God's will and not simply my own. I learned to trust Jesus, to love him, to depend on him and to walk with him in my life. I know that, if by any chance, I take the wrong way, Jesus will be with me. He will correct me, he will share his love with me and, most importantly, he will not reject me. I learned to let Jesus guide me in sad moments as well as in happy moments. "I am the servant of the Lord, let it be done to me as you say" (Luke 1:38). A life without Jesus is death; a life with Jesus is eternal life. This is the real meaning of life.

10

Hispanic Spirituality:
Perspectives of a Woman Religious

Dominga M. Zapata

Introduction

Spirituality is an integral part of every person. It is developed in and through life. A person's spirituality is recognized by the way she or he lives life. There are traces which are universal within humanity and others that are particular to a specific culture. But the spirituality of each person is marked by her/his particular life.

I will share how I have been developing a spirituality that is authentically personal and cultural through my personality, my theological formation and the events of my life's journey. There are elements which are easy to point out, while others simply fall within the mystery that is the gift of life and with little rational explanation.

This essay discusses the various stages of the personal, cultural and religious journey that has led me to a spirituality which is mine, Hispanic and at the same time Catholic. I am Minga, native Puerto Rican, the baby of a family of twelve, an immigrant to the United States, an introvert educated theologically and living as a consecrated religious. These many factors suggest that my spirituality will not be identical to that of any other Hispanic religious woman. Nevertheless, we would have some things in common because of our culture and our life style.

Cultural Aspects

The roots of my spirituality can be traced to those years in which my family survived within the giving and receiving circle of the other poor families of our neighborhood. All of our life was marked by the spirituality of our popular Catholicism which made no separation between life and religion. This was a time when we knew how to forgive and be forgiven within the vulnerability of poverty which can push one towards self-centeredness. It was a time when we learned how to depend upon the providence of God even for the necessary rain for which we begged during rogation days. It was a time when we knew how to unite with the communion of saints through an infinite number of rosaries for the dead.

This was a daily life that planted the seeds of spirituality in the absence of a Church and the sacraments. We did not depend upon the priest to bring us God. It was our mothers who exercised very well their evangelizing role. My experience confirmed the truth of the Portuguese saying: "A pinch of mothers is worth more than a pound of priests."

Then one day, like many of the pilgrim people of God, we were forced by poverty into exile. Like the family of Abraham and Sarah, my family had to leave their known land and go to the desert. I was not yet sixteen. How difficult was that experience of a young immigrant despised because of my inability to express my dreams and desires like any other young person. I was no longer at home. That life which was expressed through a known language and various cultural symbols had disappeared, together with familiar religious expressions.

Religious Aspects

I had learned in my childhood to find the sacred in the midst of the relationships with my family and community. Part of my family had remained in Puerto Rico. The Hispanic community was not sure how to relate to those who had established themselves in the United States many years ago and who had different ways of communicating and behaving.

For the first time I discovered the Church, the sacraments, and the possibility of a community of faith. These became very important because of my experience of exile and the accompanying feelings of isolation and strangeness. Once again the Lord became incarnated in the visible relationships that surrounded me. I walked in darkness like the rest of my poor immigrant people. In the suffering and oppression of my people, I discovered my vocation in life. I was to offer my entire life to God as an instrument of assurance to the people that God was indeed present in their journey. The Lord spoke clearly through life: "Leave all and follow me and I will show you how and where you must go." After my experience as an immigrant, taking a risk with my life was not so difficult for I had learned even more how to trust the God of life who had always been present to me. The spirituality I had inherited from my people helped me realize that nothing in life is accidental but rather is an expression of God's providential love. This simply was my call to religious life. It was part of the spirituality I had lived throughout my life, finding God in the concreteness of life.

The Spirituality of the Desert and of the Resurrection

Religious life has given me the grace to reflect frequently upon the journey of my life and the spirituality that sustains me. For many years of religious life, I was not aware of the roots of my own spirituality, and I tried to adopt the spirituality of my religious community. This spirituality was rooted in the dominant culture of the United States and that of the French foundress of our community. I could not figure out why I could no longer find God in prayer as I used to. The God I used to find in my prayer was the same one I found in life, in relationships, in real feelings. I was accustomed to begin my prayer time by sharing with God the joys, sorrows, and concerns that were important in my life. In the formation years of my religious life, I had to gather for prayer at a designated time and place and try to meditate aided by a book. It was an unfamiliar way of praying for me. Many years later I discovered that my spirituality was rooted in life, in the concrete, free and spontaneous relationships with God and others.

I began seeing the hand of the God who called me in the midst of the suffering and alienation of an immigrant people. It is in life, in the call of the people I serve, in my relationship with specific persons and in my interior struggle to be faithful to the message of the Kingdom, that I best find the God who has called me by my first *and* last name. My spirituality is more communitarian than individual.

Personal suffering, the pain of the poor, the agony of integration as a minority into religious life, the passion of Mother Church in her struggle to live what she proclaims, and the cry of creation waiting for its fulfillment fill up one part of my spirituality. This is what Segundo Galilea and Vicente Serrano call the spirituality of the desert.[1] For me, it is the sharing in the suffering of Christ, or as St. Paul said, "completing what is wanting. . . ." It is the part that the Hispanic people express best through their popular devotion to the Cross. These are the moments when they identify closely with their Savior because they also know what the suffering of the innocent is. During the hardest moments of my religious life, I have always had the witness of the profound tradition of the mystery of the Cross as lived by a people full of hope.

Another part of my spirituality is rooted in another aspect of the Paschal Mystery, the Resurrection. For many years, I did not know that it was precisely this. I simply knew it as *fiesta*, celebration, smiling faces, joyful perseverance, community and hope. Such experiences reminded me that every joy and success of my people is also mine, and mine are theirs. It was actually the capacity to enter into the suffering of life that made it possible to experience the resurrection.

Conclusion

Hispanic spirituality is rooted in life. To experience life is to find spirituality; it is to discover how I relate to the sacred, to others and to myself. Finding God in life has always been part of our cultural heritage. Our indigenous ancestors as well as the conquistadors have gifted us with a rich incarnational spirituality. Emmanuel is our God; God-among-us is God's name.

This is a spirituality that allows me to see God's hand in everything. Without realizing it, I became part of a community whose patroness is Mary under the title of Our Lady of Providence, the same name given her by Puerto Ricans as their patroness. It was in this context that I first learned my prayers, the numberless rosaries for the dead, which became the precursor of my religious vocation in the community of the Helpers of the Holy Souls in Purgatory (known as the Society of Helpers) whose charism is to pray, work and suffer for the souls in purgatory.

These are some of the essential components of a spirituality that is transformed through the desert and the resurrection of every Hispanic religious woman. The details are different but the fundamentals of religious life and the incarnation of Christ are the pillars inherited from our spiritual tradition reflected in the lives of our great saints, as well as in the lives of the people, poor and humble.

Finding God among the suffering people is the desert. Letting us be captivated by God among the people is the resurrection. The Hispanic religious woman manifests her spirituality by emptying her heart in prayer, thus permitting her to contemplate the same God in the history of the people; in knowing how to interpret life in the light of faith; in recognizing the God of history; in knowing what to do with and for those oppressed by sin; in living out her beliefs; and in constantly actualizing the final judgement message of Matthew 25:31-46 where Jesus is seen in the hungry, naked and imprisoned. Life is received as the gratuitous gift of the God of our fathers and mothers given anew to each person.

I conclude this reflection on Hispanic spirituality from my perspective as a woman religious with the words used at the celebration of my jubilee by a people who have also witnessed this greatness:

> Before you were born, I knew you,
> I knew your name; therefore I called you.
> To give witness of my love
> I filled you with my gifts and graces.[2]

NOTES

1. Segundo Galilea, ed. *El Seguimiento de Cristo* (Bogotá: Paulinas, 1981). Vicente Serrano. *Espiritualidad del Desierto* (Madrid: Studium, 1968).

2. Cf. Jeremiah 1:4-5.

11

"It's Great
That We Are Getting Older"

Silvia Zaldívar

The expression "It's great that we are getting older" must seem like a contradiction to those who, following the popular wisdom and the most accepted theories, see old age as the time of life in which we are declining in health and activity; the ailments of these years mean that no one is happy to see them arrive. In the United States especially, youth is worshipped. The advertising of products for looking younger represents millions of dollars, and at the fatal age of sixty-five a person is considered a senior citizen, words which don't mean anything literally but which carry, like a stigma, the idea that we are no longer a part of the productive life of work, or of the family or, unfortunately, of the Church. From this point on we will be seen merely as a problem, or as someone dependent who should receive with resignation the crumbs which society offers in the form of a very small government check, or a visit to the old folks' home by the students of a confirmation class or a telephone call on Mother's or Father's Day.

It is not the same in the spiritual life. The development of that soul saved by the precious blood of Jesus Christ continues until the day it returns to its Creator.

Bernice Neugarten (professor emerita of the department of behavioral sciences at the University of Chicago) says that "years ago it was believed that one grew to an adult age and after age forty-five one began to decline. This happens only if one considers bone structure, but in reality, the person grows in wisdom, charity and love towards others until the end of life.''

There is an international organization founded in France called *La Vie Montante* (Ascendant Life) which has as its objective to support the spiritual growth of persons of advanced age. Its philosophy is the same which we have expressed earlier. Human beings neither decline nor deteriorate; on the contrary, they accumulate riches in their faith, which is seen more objectively and more meaningfully as they gain experience, gifts and years. Life is like a wheel; its circle is not complete until it goes all the way around, and if the circle is not complete it can't fulfill its mission, which is to move the vehicle.

Stages of Development

In order to understand this theory better, let's think about our own lives and the various stages through which we pass in the spiritual life in order to complete the circle, and just like the wheel, to move our soul:

1. We begin with the process of feeling God within ourselves (introduction of the child/young person into the faith);
2. Upon sensing God, Creator and Redeemer, in our own lives we feel the desire and need to worship God (devotions, liturgy); and
3. Upon reaching the fullness of this faith we need to pass it on to others (ministry, service).

We remember our first emotions as children at prayer, later at our First Communion and the many Communions that followed. I myself have a vivid memory of my paternal grandmother, with whom I spent a lot of time when we lived in Caibarién, the port city in Cuba where I was born, especially when my brother was born and my mother was very busy. My grandma made me repeat with her the morning and afternoon prayers, and she spoke to me about God and the Virgin Mary. She and my mother used to take me to Mass at the School of the Apostolate, the house of a religious order of Cuban sisters who recently marked their one-hundredth anniversary there;[1] praying instilled in me the love of God as they felt it. I began to experience it as a reflection of my love for my family, but that was only the foundation which prepared me for my own independent spiritual life.

Some years later my parents moved to Havana, and since I was of high school age they inquired about schools near our new house. By miraculous coincidence, there was a religious high school a few steps from the house which turned out to be affiliated with the one I used to go to with my grandmother in Caibarién. It was God's plan that the nuns should continue to guide me and . . . that's when I had my first encounter with Jesus. I remember the eve of my First Communion when I found myself in the school chapel, and I realized that I was communicating with the Supreme Being and that it was no longer through my grandma or mother, nor through the sisters. That was the beginning of my spiritual life.

In the same way that little ones need help to develop physically, they also need our support for their spiritual development, and we all remember those people who initiated us in the faith: the catechist, the sister at school, and above all our parents and grandparents. For that reason it is so important that the evangelization of the child not end with the First Communion, since that is only the beginning. Those who have already "risen" higher in their lives are a very valuable resource in the process of turning the wheel of life.

"Let the little children come to Me," Jesus said. We could change that saying to: "Let the grandparents bring Me closer to the little ones."

When that identification with God becomes part of our being, we want to show it. Therefore, the second phase of this process is usually through devotions, that is, chances to talk to God and to be involved with that spiritual expression which is so much a part of our lives, as is the acceptance of the Virgin Mary and the saints as mediators or intercessors between ourselves and the three divine persons of the Trinity.

The third phase which we recognize in spiritual development is service to others. The Apostle James in his letter (2:14-18) asks what good it does to say that we have faith if we do not show it with our deeds. The meaning of "faith" as used by the apostle in his letter is the same meaning we give it today, intellectual assent to a series of doctrines based on the truth proclaimed by the Church and summarized in the Creed that we pray every Sunday and which is the center of the sacraments which strengthen us as Christians. It is not the doctrines by themselves that make us Christians. Rather, it is the example we give by our lives and through our constant dedication to serving others and to sharing that faith through our love even to our enemies, serving them both in their material and spiritual needs.

In his letter St. James complements the idea of faith of St. Paul, who considers faith to be a complete commitment to God through the crucified and risen Jesus. Pauline faith tells us that we are going to God, and St. James tells us that we are already with God.

According to St. James, we are not demonstrating a love for others when we judge them ourselves or when we help only those we like or those we think are deserving; in a word, we are merely practicing charity in a way which is easy and comfortable for us, without risking our own well-being.

Those of us who have been blessed with long life, and I say this from personal experience, see these feelings change as the years pass and we become less and less focused on our own individual beliefs and devotions.

An example proves this:

Some years ago I led a group of older people to Europe. The agency that arranged the trip sold too many tickets. This caused me and six others to have to go by another route, which turned out to be filled with problems and obstacles. After spending three days in the New York airport without leaving for Spain, we decided to try to return to Chicago, and we first gathered to say a prayer to ask the Holy Spirit to guide our footsteps.

One of the older women in the group who had a vivid idea of Christian charity said: "Lord, first of all, we pray that we might not feel anger or bitterness against those who, acting dishonestly, have put us in this situation." This petition was not the one which a young person would probably have made: "Lord, grant that we might make the trip to Europe." No, her thought reflected the maturity of her spiritual life.

Culture Shock

But what happens when, because of migration to other countries, we are in an environment dominated by a culture in which the process of spiritual development occurs in a way different from what we saw in our ancestors?

In the first phase we see that our grandchildren, if they came very young or were born here, adapt more easily in the world around them, but they encounter culture shock in their homes and in their older relatives.

The second phase involves the dedication to worship, but it is not easy for us to practice it not only because of the language barrier but more than anything else because of differences in customs. We have an obligation to pray in the parish, that is, in the church that is near us geographically. I must register in that parish and regularly give the expected financial contribution, which I am not accustomed to do. Our customs follow the ecclesiology of the "sanctuary." In my country I attended wherever my devotion took me, recognizing that we are all part of the Mystical Body of Christ and it doesn't matter who might be sitting next to me in the church pew, where I feel like a stranger and not part of the community.

In the third stage, when one feels a powerful desire to share Christian love and fellowship with others, I find myself alone because the ideal in this country is that an elderly person live an independent life without social interaction other than that at the senior center or the Legion of Mary one hour a week. When I recall the respect and love my grandparents enjoyed, and even the financial security they had because they were not cut off from society at a certain age, I feel a bit wistful. I channel that into a desire to change customs and allow the older people in our communities and parishes, no matter where they were born or grew up, to enjoy a third stage of the spiritual life. In this stage they need not pray alone or be satisfied with watching Mass on television because they can't get to church. Their moral and spiritual values can be an example and inspiration to their younger family members, neighbors, and friends.

I recognize that it is very difficult to combine two cultures, and even more so to exchange our own culture for another, but we can offer what is valuable from our own roots, continuing to practice our own customs, religious traditions and language, while at the same time trying to recognize and appreciate what other cultures have to offer. For example, one day which is seldom celebrated among Hispanics is Grandparents' Day, which in this country is celebrated on the second Sunday of September. One of the most beautiful traditions in the United States is Thanksgiving, but for us it is simply a free day and we even call it "Turkey Day," depriving the name of the holiday of its lovely meaning which is to give thanks for God's blessings and for the love of those around us. Holy Week has for us the connotation of grief, of sadness, while in Anglo society the Resurrection is celebrated from the very beginning of the week and the Passion and Death of Jesus are simply the means which allow us to celebrate his triumph. When it comes to the death of a loved one, we express our pain of loss more vehemently than what we see in Anglo funerals, where an atmosphere of spiritual peace shows a sense of hope and faith in a happy afterlife. All these examples demonstrate cultural values which could broaden our spiritual life if we analyze them and integrate them into our lives.

Conclusion

If we start from the sociological principle that human beings are social and cannot live in isolation, and if we add the reflections offered in this article about the need to share our faith with others, then we should change the conditions of the third stage of the spiritual life for the elderly in this country. We should work toward the fulfillment of the two commandments which are the foundation of Christianity: Love God, and love one another. In that way we would allow all people to be able to develop their spirituality in whichever stage of life they find themselves and in whatever place on earth they happen to be living.

NOTE

1. In December, 1991, I had the good fortune to attend the commemoration of the one-hundredth anniversary of the founding of the Institute of Cuban Sisters of the Apostolate of the Sacred Heart of Jesus, the school where I received my education from first grade to high school. Reflecting during the celebration about the influence of the sisters on my life, I thought about how much I must thank God for those who guided my steps in the spiritual life during the three stages of my life: my mother, my grandmother, the sisters of the Apostolate, the Cuban Catholic Action Youth Group, and my husband and my children.

12

The Spirituality of a Hispanic Family

José and Mercedes Rivera

In a dehumanizing, mass consumer society, many people see marriage devalued because of the erosion of moral values and spiritual principles. But it is now time to think about those of us for whom this reality of Christian marriage is meaningful and valuable. We are searching with great longing for a spirituality of marriage that might bring us closer to God and to each other.

All of the faithful are called to the fullness of Christian life and charity. Married love provides many ways, circumstances and opportunities for couples to follow the call to holiness. Married love is the form of human love that most closely mirrors the love of Christ for the Church. Through baptism and the sacrament of marriage, we have the privilege of exercising our priesthood within the context of the family and of being connected to Our Lord Jesus Christ.

When we entered into marriage some thirty years ago, premarital preparation programs did not exist in El Salvador, our native country. Today there is the Pre-Cana Program, which is a service offered by various dioceses and in which both of us serve willingly and lovingly.

At the time when we made the most important decision that two human beings can make by entering into a marriage in the Church, we were not fully conscious of the seriousness of this commitment because we were so young (Mercedes was nineteen and José was twenty). We had absolutely no idea of the importance of the sacrament of marriage, since in an environment where machismo predominates marriage was seen as something negative. Whenever someone would get married, people would say that he had hung himself or they would make jokes like: "One less virgin and one more Christ."

Perhaps the decision to enter the sacrament of marriage was made because of tradition or due to particular circumstances. In our case Mercedes was pregnant when we got married. If we didn't formalize our relationship, she ran the risk of losing her job. At that time it was an embarrassment for any business to have an unmarried pregnant employee. We ask ourselves now: Is this good or bad? Is it a serious prejudice? Or is it a way to make young people take responsibility?

After four months our first child, Vilma Sonia, was born. Beforehand we had gotten our hopes up that the baby would be a boy. We had not yet learned that our Lord does not grant wishes to people, but rather that things happen according to his will. Mercedes felt very disappointed that she hadn't pleased José in this way. When he arrived at the maternity hospital to see her, she said: "I couldn't please you. It was a girl."

José, impatient and excited, asked the nurse to take him to see his daughter. When he took her in his arms, he felt that special emotion that only the birth of one's child gives to a person. Then he went back to Mercedes and thanked her and our Lord for giving us such a beautiful and healthy baby.

A year passed and José was still dreaming of the son who would carry on his name. That's when Mirna, our beautiful and healthy second daughter, was born. We talked about it and agreed to have a third child, and that time our son José was born. Mercedes felt so blessed by the Lord that she had been able to satisfy her husband's hope. José felt proud and fulfilled, more a man than ever, and we gave thanks to God for listening to us.

At age two our son developed a severe allergy. He suffered not only from very high fevers but also from open sores that broke out in his face. Liquid oozed from the sores, and wherever it touched it caused another sore. His back and arms also became cracked and sore. The child was very brave and didn't cry, but just moaned and put his little arm over his face. We were constantly sitting on the edge of his bed and applying the medicine that the doctors recommended. Sharing our son's pain, we would cry bitterly and pray with all our hearts and with tremendous faith that the Lord would provide the means for our son to be cured. Once again the Lord heard our pleas and the miracle came about through a neighbor. She asked our permission to take the child to the Benjamin Blun Children's Hospital where a specialist in that type of disease saw him. The doctor told Mercedes: "Mrs. Rivera, don't worry any more. Your son will be cured of this disease." Thanks to God, the child was indeed cured.

Without knowing it, we were living our spirituality of marriage. We shared the pain and we witnessed to a Christ of life and hope. We didn't lose our faith in him. Our Father's love for us is so great that he always listens to us when we pray from the heart. That's how much we as parents love our children, so much so that when they are sick we would prefer to suffer their sickness and pain.

The sacrament of marriage has been given to us so that we might witness to Christ in our hearts, as individuals and as a couple. In that way we create a conjugal and family-oriented dimension. We struggle every day to make Christ the center of our lives, by confidently sharing our sorrows and joys, and by being better friends every day. We make sure that we have between us kindness, esteem, respect, and acceptance. All of this flows into the river of holiness. That is what the spirituality of marriage is all about.

We spent many years not knowing all of these spiritual riches and not being able to find the road that led to happiness. The only road that led us to happiness was getting closer to God. Now we see our married life with different eyes. We have completely changed our way of life. Of course we are careful not to go to fanatical extremes, and we are still happy and sociable people.

Thanks to God, we never go to bed angry or resentful, even though we might have had some problems or differences of opinion, since that is an inevitable part of life. Married people who say that they don't have problems are not really living. The real accomplishment lies in having difficulties and knowing how to work them out in an intelligent and Christian way.

For us it hasn't been easy to achieve this focus on marriage and family. We both know perfectly well that we have to give one-hundred percent in our daily lives. Only in that way can problems, no matter how difficult, become easier and the joyful moments deeper. We are very conscious of the fact that we must keep ourselves close to our Lord because every marriage that moves away from God tends to fall apart. We say this with good reason and from our own experience: after exactly eighteen years of marriage we broke up and even got a legal divorce. We each built our own personal hell, which was the product of our moving away from God. Pride, selfishness, and the interference of third parties (given that the only third party who should be between us is Christ) led us to this destruction.

We were separated for five years and our break-up caused pain and unpleasant consequences. Our children were at the age when they most needed our support and guidance. Our son José loved us very much and used to admire us as parents. We were his idols and role models. But when his role models came crashing down, he felt empty, confused, and depressed. Looking for some cure for his pain, he started trying to fill that emptiness by using drugs. The habit is both harmful and progressive and by the time he was eighteen it had taken control of him. Drugs were more powerful than his willpower.

We tried everything humanly possible to help him in his recovery. Sometimes we felt like we couldn't go on. Only God could return to us our son who was lost to drug addiction. We put him in the hands of the Lord, and we started to pray every night. As a couple we prayed to our Lord with all our faith and hope. Little by little, our son began to respond and recover. He started to distance himself from the friends with whom he no longer had anything in common. Last year he moved to Alaska where our oldest daughter lives. Now, thanks be to God, he is a new and better man.

Despite the wrong road that our son had traveled, there was always a spiritual flame flickering in him, and that was our hope. In his room he always kept a Christ, a figure of Jesus of Atocha, and an image of the Virgin Mary.

These symbols are impressed upon us for a lifetime and with them our whole way of being and our multi-faceted spirituality. For us Latins the most important thing is unity. We are very expressive and communicative. That human warmth that brings us close to others is what characterizes us. We possess a great resource in our cultural tradition. We celebrate the Blessed Virgin on several feast days and with great enthusiasm. That is where the spirituality of Latin families comes from. We have an immense folklore to offer in this country. We have traditions we can share with other cultures without feeling ashamed or unworthy.

Right now in our family we never tire of giving constant thanks to God for having such a close family. Although our children live far away, there is always communication and a network of prayer among us. Sonia, our oldest daughter and the mother of four children, lives in Alaska. We sometimes spend Christmas with them. On those occasions we thoroughly enjoy the warmth of family, as we tell jokes and play with the children. Mercedes lovingly prepares delicious meals, always preceded by family prayer. All of this is family spirituality.

This Christmas we will go to Puerto Rico where our daughter Mirna, who now has two children, lives. The days seem long as we wait for the chance to be together and share some time with them. It is beautiful to be married for twenty, thirty, and why not, fifty years if God wills it, and to be able to see the children grow and develop and then to enjoy the grandchildren who gladden the hearts of us, their grandparents. It is our responsibility to struggle for family unity because that is God's plan.

In the spirituality of Hispanic families, it doesn't make sense to us that our children should simply leave home when they are no longer minors or when they get married. We always long to have them nearby. What makes even less sense is the notion that the grandparents should be shut up in nursing homes. Instead we benefit tremendously from their presence and feel great respect and love for them. This spirituality identifies and characterizes us.

We struggle so that our family doesn't lose those human, spiritual family values now that we are in this country. This, of course, requires effort and sacrifice because the environment outside the home is quite different and, in some instances, harmful to our values. Therefore, we should take advantage of all the resources offered by our Catholic Church that are appropriate to today's needs.

We have found the means necessary to re-educate ourselves as a family within the Christian Family Movement, since it provides services like Marriage Encounters, Marriage Returns, Son and Daughter Encounters, Single Parent Family Groups, and various stages of Growth Groups. This collection of groups is like rain falling down from heaven on all the Catholic families of goodwill. This is the place where we have heard our Lord's call to share our experiences humbly with others and to learn from others every day. There are none so poor that they have nothing to give, and there are none so rich as to have nothing to learn from others. In the way of the Lord everything is reciprocal, and it is in giving that we receive. In order for the Lord to pour out his grace on us, we have to die each day to selfishness and pride. What gives us joy is breathing life into our daily lives as a Christian family. That's how we go about continuing the work which our Lord Jesus Christ began for us.

13

The Spirituality of a Deacon

Enrique D. Alonso

How true is the phrase: "There's no better book than life itself." I would add: "When one lives that life attentively and deeply." This takes me back to my childhood to recall the teaching of my parents and of those many others who contributed to my formation in the faith. Throughout all these years I have continued to value all of those lessons which have helped in the development of my spirituality.

I was born in San Luis Potosí, Mexico, a stately and profoundly religious city. Spirituality was in the air: in the bells which called people to Mass starting at five in the morning, in the feast days of each neighborhood's patron saint, in the various religious Orders present in their churches, and in the religious festivals celebrated by all the faithful throughout the year. In March was Holy Week together with the Procession of Silence; in May was the feast of the Holy Cross; in July, the Virgin of Carmen celebrated with a procession of bullfighters; in August, the celebrations of St. Louis of France, the patron saint of the city, and the feast of the Assumption; in October, the visit of the Virgin of Guadalupe to other churches; in November, All Soul's Day and the feast of St. Cecilia, patroness of musicians; and from December to February, all of the festivities associated with the Virgin of Guadalupe and the Christmas season: the *Posadas*, the *Acostada*, Epiphany and the *Levantada*, and the feast of Candlemas. This was the atmosphere in which I grew up.

I was the youngest of seven children, and I arrived eight years after the next-to-youngest of my siblings. This may have contributed to an increased awareness of what was happening around me, since I practically grew up as an only child. I received my first religious instruction from my mother, who taught me to make the Sign of the Cross and to say my evening prayers: "Angel of God, my Guardian dear . . . do not forsake me by night or by day, nor leave me alone to lose my way." With her I learned to pray the Hail Mary at dawn and at the hour of the Angelus. With her I learned about the lives of the saints and the prayers of the novenas.

Now that I can analyze it, I realize that it was my father who taught me who God was. Through him I learned the concept of God as Father, a Father who was attentive to the needs of his children. I learned of the relationship that existed among us as people, since he taught me to pray for those who were more in need than I. I learned from my father that God was the Creator of all that I could see, and he showed me how God was the Architect *par excellence*, since everything had been perfectly calculated, from the stars in the sky to the hills and the animals, to the human organism. I learned that all this was part of creation and that as long as everything stayed in harmony—since that was the way God had created it—we would be able to have a better life. That is to say, we could not go against the ways that God had created things.

It is only now that I can appreciate the wisdom of my parents, especially since neither of them completed more than four years of school. I can also appreciate how deeply involved they were in life through their beliefs and traditions. It is only now that I can appreciate the quality of life that they had and the quality of life that they gave us, even though our financial situation was precarious. Perhaps it was for that reason that I always lived with the hope of a gift from the infant Jesus because I knew that my parents wouldn't be able to provide one.

I learned my catechism from an old woman in the neighborhood who gathered the neighborhood children together on Saturday afternoons to teach us the basics of the faith. Everything had to be memorized and, in order to make this easier, we had to sing it in unison to whatever tune she gave us. I remember the first lines of the lesson. "Every faithful Christian is obliged to have heartfelt devotion. . . ." It was the same thing with: "The Commandments of God are ten: . . .

you shall not kill, you shall not commit adultery, you shall not use the name of God in vain. . . .'' Every month at the parish we met with the children of another neighborhood in order to learn about the Church, and we were given candy. How we loved those days! After making our First Communion all together, the altar boys who would serve the priests during Sunday Mass were chosen. For that we had to learn how to answer the priest in Latin.

These were my first years of religious formation, and how much they have helped me during the course of my life! How many times through the ups and downs of my life have I been able to hold on to these treasures in order not to lose my way, my patience or my faith! How many times in the process of my formation have I had to return to them as points of reference in order not to lose sight of the wisdom of faith!

The second part of my formation took place in Chicago in my young adulthood. With the drastic life change that occurs upon immigrating to this country, in addition to the trauma of a change of environment and language, I lost my sense of relationship to authority. That is to say, I no longer felt responsible to anyone. Now I depended on my own judgment. Suddenly I had all this space and all this freedom and did not know what to do with it. I learned everything at once, by falling down and getting back up again.

After enjoying this new situation for a while and learning from mistakes, that sense of a lack of direction returned to my life. Searching for an answer, I participated in a Christian *cursillo*. This was one of the most powerful experiences of my adult life, in which I encountered Jesus. Not the Jesus of the manger or that child Jesus lost in the temple or the one from the prayer to the Sacred Heart, but rather a living Jesus, risen, real, walking with his Church among human beings with their problems and longings, suffering, rejoicing and celebrating with us.

After that encounter I learned all of these things little by little in the process of my maturation as a Christian. From that came my understanding of and desire for mission. From that came my desire to proclaim the Jesus whom many people don't know. Though I never thought that I could speak in public, I began to prepare myself to spread that message by means of a school of the community of *los Hermanos de la familia de Dios*, who gave me the opportunity to go into the streets, to knock on doors, and to learn about the worries, suffering, grief, and fear of the Hispanic immigrants in this country.

Through this I learned how these brothers and sisters were able to see Jesus in their lives through us. They could speak with that trust and security that comes from knowing that they were talking to one like them, since together with the brother who was listening to them was Jesus, in whom they regained hope. This is because faith was demonstrated in the openness that they had toward us, who were strangers to them. So, little by little, there came the Masses in Spanish, and the chance for them to profess their faith and recognize themselves as valuable persons in their environment. Little by little, many of these people started going to the *cursillos*, to *los Hermanos*, and to the mission, and taking history into their own hands. We know the rest.

When I was in one of those moments in which life demands that we define ourselves, I found myself very much drawn to the missions. I even made some inquiries to the Maryknoll Fathers. Whether because of chance or because of fate, I had to return to my country for an emergency, and it was then that I met Juanita, my wife. It was one of those things that was meant to be. A few months later we were married in order to share our lives forever.

Juanita is a spiritual woman with a definite religious foundation. Her parents were involved in very traditional apostolic movements of the Church such as *las Hijas de María y la Adoración Nocturna*. Since Juanita was educated in a school run by religious sisters, she has been for me a perfect example of what Church tradition is all about. I go to her to find out where this or that tradition came from or what certain symbols mean. For example, from her I learned of the relationship between the presentation of girls in the church when they reach age three and the Presentation of Mary by her parents at the same age.

A few years after I was married, I was called to participate in the permanent diaconate. In the beginning I wasn't sure that this was for me. Not because I didn't want to commit myself to the Church more than I already was, but rather because I didn't consider myself worthy of the call. With the support of Juanita, I was able to understand that the Lord was calling me for something beyond what I had done up to then. For one thing, the diaconate provided me with the foundation of knowledge about our faith that I had not previously had regarding the Scriptures, the liturgy, and the sacraments; knowledge that enriches preaching, the prayers of the faithful and the celebrations of the sacraments. In addition, the diaconate came to enrich our married life.

After ordination there has been a process of formation to deepen what I had learned until then, both in knowledge and in spirituality. All of this has led me to a more intimate relationship with God through the Liturgy of the Hours, the Rosary, meditation, Mass, and meetings with *los Hermanos*—moments in which I am conscious of the presence of God. They also happen in the family when we pray before meals, give thanks or ask a favor of God, in our family celebrations on Thanksgiving, in the Christmas season, on All Souls' Day or on Easter Sunday.

These experiences have led me to respect and value the presence of the risen Jesus among us in all my activities with groups of the faithful whether through teaching, the liturgy, or in community planning. In this I recognize what I learned with *los Hermanos de la familia de Dios* when they say that the voice of the people is the voice of God.

We are a people of celebrations, relationships, and traditions. I don't know if we are different from others, but I do know that we do not need a specific place in order to encounter the mystery of God. We encounter this mystery even in our dead relatives, who continue to be a part of our lives and our celebrations. We remember them in all of our prayers. By remembering them they become present in those moments of conversation.

In these difficult times in our world, when institutional values are falling one by one, and moral values have become so distorted, when the questions of our faith seem so fragile and credibility is decreasing, I go back to the basics, to that which is fundamental in our religious life: prayer and the conviction that God will provide. What is sometimes missing, however, is our willingness to cooperate with the God who provides all that we need. I know that we have a lot of work to do to awaken us to this change of life and heart and to put ourselves back into contact with creation, with ourselves, and with God. That is the only way that we can save our world and our way of life. In the process, I know that I have my space and my sanctuary for finding God and strengthening my spirit and my faith. I can do it in my home and in the community of faith. God is in the community!

14

Re-discovering My Spiritual History: Exodus and Exile

Alvaro Dávila

It is appropriate to say at the beginning of this essay that my purpose is not to define the spirituality of the Latin American male, but rather to talk about it in one of its dimensions: its historical reality. It seems to me that spiritual experience can only be recognized, reflected upon, and understood when we live in continuous dialogue with the memories of a people. Trying to define the essence of life without this dialogue would result in an incomplete reality.

I will confine this discussion to the historical dimension. Even so, I believe that this discussion will serve as a motivation for more detailed studies about some realities which I hope to sketch out. I will attempt to recover some of the reasons why my people tried to break with a history that has given us life and which has inspired us to get where we are today. We have proudly learned that both Spirit and People are realities only when one is present with them and is a part of them.

As a Latin American living far from my native country, I remember and relive much of what makes me who I am today. I have learned to admit that my parents did not have the chance to finish elementary school. My mother, a peasant woman and an expert in natural medicine, had her first child (my oldest brother) at age fifteen; my father was orphaned at age six, and from that time on he had to work in order to survive. Unfortunately I don't know much about my grandparents, but the circumstances of my father and my mother already give me an idea of the reality from which I come.

I think of my mother, a country woman, who is wise and respectful of nature and who knows a lot about herbal medicines; she understands herbs not only for curing people but also for helping animals, but because she didn't finish primary school she feels ignorant next to her son for whom she sacrificed to pay the costs of high school. Today as I finish a master's degree in pastoral studies, I have to do exercises like writing these lines to be able to realize the wisdom of my mother and my people whom for many decades I put down and considered ignorant.

I think of my father who always introduces himself as an "Automobile Pilot." I always imagined that it is because he is ashamed to admit that he was a chauffeur, that he hasn't gone to school, that he isn't a "professional." But the truth is that he says he is an automobile pilot not out of shame, but out of pride. This is his "profession." It is the job by means of which he honestly earned the few cents which enabled my brothers, sisters and me to eat, buy clothes, and go out. But I was going to school and one day I would be a professional, and for that reason I couldn't understand what he meant by "Automobile Pilot." It took me more than twenty years to discover that my father is a historian, mason, carpenter, mechanic, electrician, architect, and a welder. He designed and, with my mother, built the house where they live to this day. But he also did not complete elementary school. One thing for sure, my father, like so many men of his generation, still tips his hat to greet people.

In their kindness and love for five daughters and four sons, my father and mother, trying to prevent history from repeating itself, always pushed us to "be more than they were," even though for all their trouble what I learned was to be something that I am not.

Remembering and accepting our own history teaches us the violence that is done to our lives when, upon entering a technical academic world, we are stripped, or we have to strip ourselves of our roots, of what we are. It is not often in academic life that we are given the tools to discover, affirm and celebrate our identity as God's creatures in a particular place and time.

The world outside the home is filled with ideas and attitudes which don't allow us to be who we are. I get a lump in my throat when I remember the times in school when I hid to eat my "bread and beans" which my mother used to prepare for me so lovingly at 4:00 in the morning. I knew that my schoolmates, who were as poor as I was, brought "ham sandwiches" (at least that's what they said). I remember that they used to say to me: "You bring bread with black chicken," as a way of making fun of me.

Our experience has been a struggle marked by rejection. The price of that struggle is sometimes our human dignity itself, which breaks our spirit. We get to a point at which, unconsciously, it is no longer possible to communicate with God in the language, culture, or circumstances which God so graciously gave us. It is very sad to remember, because in those memories there exists a constant denial of ourselves. Might it be that at some moment in history something happened which should never have happened?

The result is that today when I look at all my academic preparation, at the fact that in order to talk about my mother and father I don't use a pencil but rather a computer, I realize that I don't know a fraction of what they knew at my age. That's because in my academic formation I was told that in order to learn in this world I would have to learn how to operate certain machines that would help me to write, and I would need to quote other people, people foreign to my history; that I should have read a certain amount of foreign literature, and I never had to read *Popol Vuh* (the holy book of the Mayas) as part of my education. This would have helped me to understand better why I eat so many tortillas, corn stew, tamales and corn drinks. Who knows, I might have even considered becoming a farmer and learned to respect Mother Nature. But instead I had to eat ham sandwiches in school to be considered "normal." Only the rejected, the poor, the Indian or the lowly, as we tend to describe them, eat tortillas and beans.

Now that I remember, it brings tears to my eyes when I hear my mother, with her immense unconditional love, telling me so often not to say that she was my mother, so that I wouldn't feel tied to a "peasant reality," which in the capital city would only serve to make me part of a rejected heritage and which would prevent me from advancing "in the civilized world of the Ladinos." In fact, I even learned to insult others by saying, "You look like an Indian."

I remember the tears in my father's eyes when I took down all his photos from his living room wall and put them in a box sealed with tape and tied with twine, as if to make sure that they wouldn't get out. I was ashamed of them when my school friends came to visit me. Those time-yellowed photographs reflect the little that my father knows of his history. They show the faces of the people who helped my father and the efforts that he had made to "get ahead" in his life. They speak of the suffering of being orphaned, but also of the joys and the pride of being father of a family of nine. Today my father has those same photos on the walls of his room. Every time I go home those pictures remind me of what I did.

Mine is a history of constant denial of what I am, a *mestizo* with a beard, the product of a raped Indian culture who has had to spend most of his life denying who he is. Finally, after being confronted, I have begun to recognize the identity that "Tata Chus" (Father of Jesus) gave me.

My background has helped me to learn to value what we often deny. I remember that when I arrived in the United States and I began to wash dishes, I felt so happy the first day because I was working. But as the days went by, it became depressing to realize that this was what I would do for the rest of my life. But what else could I do? I came to this country to work.

Then, after my first week of work, they couldn't pay me because they didn't have my Social Security number to make out the check. In my naïvete I told them: "Just make out the check to my name and that's enough." They responded: "Don't be a . . . it's not your name we care about, but your number." How sad, I said to myself! In order to be someone in life it is not enough just to quit being rural, to stop eating beans, to have no mother, but now not even my name mattered. I could go by any name, since it no longer made any difference.

In the midst of all this rejection something happened. It was during Advent in 1986 in our parish (Nuestra Señora de la Merced in Chicago). We were invited those four Sundays to wear the typical clothing of our countries. It was something very colorful, wonderful, and joyful to see a whole world of people arrive each Sunday who were celebrating their life, with their colors, their clothing and the fragrance that those give off, and all of it in the name of the God who gave us that life, that face, that fragrance and that color.

Suddenly, just like when children discover their shadows and see themselves without realizing that it is them, I asked myself two questions: First, on this occasion not only the children dressed in their special clothing, but so did the adults. That didn't happen in our native countries. We had never wanted to be indigenous people. The only time indigenous dress was allowed during the religious celebration of the town was for the festivals of the Virgin of Guadalupe, for which the boys and girls dressed as "Little Indians," but the adults never dressed up. What was happening here, I asked myself? We were celebrating what we had rejected our entire lives. How is that possible?

A second and more profound question occurred to me later. I started thinking that my people, when they came to this country, brought with them those indigenous things that they had rejected for generations. It didn't matter how many rivers we had to cross; it didn't matter that we had never worn them; it didn't matter that we might never wear them. Nevertheless we brought them with us and we hung them up on the walls of our homes, and we gave them to our new neighbors in other countries as a sign of our love for them. How can it be that we would bring that which we rejected, I asked myself? My answer was laughter, pleasure, and also anxiety. I trembled because I saw my children dressed up like "Tona," the Indian woman who used to sell me corn drink every day. I trembled because I didn't know what was happening.

Years after that experience I realize that our life, along with our language, with our medicinal plants, with our good customs, with its beautiful and rich culture, this life is good enough to enable us to be in harmony with God and with God's creation. Today I have learned to be free. Today I have learned to be spiritual because I have reconnected with my roots, with the source of my life. Today I have a clearer idea of where I'm going. Today I have learned to call myself a child of God. Today I have learned to see God in my brothers and sisters, and although I don't wear a hat with which I could greet people respectfully as my father does, I have learned to stand up and give them my hand.

That's why when I was asked to write my experience of spirituality as a Latin American man, as the Christian I profess to be, the word "conversion" came to mind. Conversion to what, I asked myself? Well, being a man I was told that I would be the provider for a family, and for that reason I had to go to school and educate myself and learn. For that reason I do believe that to speak of the spirituality of the Latin American male is also to speak of conversion. The only difference is that this time we are talking about a conversion to recognize ourselves as God made us.

Through writing this article I have stopped being dead. I have gone from death to life. My story was dead, and now it has come to life. Blessed be God, my mother, my father, and all of us, God's people.

15

"Dear Father Arturo"

Clotilde Olvera Márquez

Dear Father Arturo,

That afternoon when you called to invite me to write something about the spirituality of the Hispanic woman I joyfully said to myself: "Yes, I will try." And here I am trying. I don't know when you read these pages if you will find what you asked for or what you want. I do know that I'm going to do it lovingly, asking God to enlighten me. Since I consider you a good friend, I confess to you that I am just as impulsive in all of my decisions: I am one of those who speaks first and thinks afterward. But until now I have not regretted acting this way because the Lord always accompanies me if it relates to my faith, my Church, or an act of service.

I also want you to know that I felt very flattered. And why not: at my age there aren't many who pay attention to us since, according to popular opinion, we're no longer good for anything and are pushed aside. Many are taken to nursing homes and hospitals with the excuse that they're going to be taken care of. This is one of the customs that I still can't accept. In my culture old people are loved and cared for.

Years ago my niece's mother-in-law died at age 115. She was like a little baby who was spoon fed and had to have her diapers changed. Naturally, my niece felt tired, though I never heard her complain. Every time I visited them, I marvelled at the love with which they treated her. What surprised me even more was that at a certain time in the afternoon that little old woman called everyone by name and went around singing old songs of praise.

Throughout the story which I am telling there will be testimonies like this one so that you might understand that when I arrived in this country I suffered a tremendous shock. I'm not exaggerating. The reason is that I was born and grew up in an atmosphere of deeply-rooted piety. I was born in León, Guanajuato, Mexico, on June 3, 1912. When I was eight days old I was baptized with the name María Clotilde de la Luz. Clotilde was for the saint's day on which I was born, and María de la Luz, for the image of the Virgin Mary—most holy patron of the city—which is especially venerated in the León Cathedral.

My mother was a very devout woman who left her children the legacy of a great faith. By her example and teachings we learned to believe in God, to love Mary, our Blessed Mother. She also instilled in us a great respect for priests and for the elderly, and she taught us to have compassion for the needy by taking food or clothing to our poorest neighbors. I have always believed that during the Christmas season her greatest joy was in seeing us children scramble noisily to get the fruit, sweets, and candies of the *piñata*. In order to participate in all of this, we first had to pay attention during The Rosary and the novena. In addition, the toys we received on the Feast of Epiphany depended on our behavior during those nights. She used to tell us that she was the one responsible for letting the Wise Men know how we were behaving ourselves. In the end no one was left without a toy. My mother saw to that. My father, just to make her mad, jokingly called her a fanatic. I think that today's world needs fanatics like her. In my memory this was the most beautiful period of my life.

I was fifteen when my mother died. There were two tragedies which affected her deeply: the León flood of 1926 and the *Cristero* revolution, which broke out in January 1927. For that reason I say now and I will always say: "I have seen the affliction of my people, I have heard their cries" (Exod 3:7-8). Sometimes in reviewing the long history of humanity, we come across moments that can truly be classified as historic. The excuse which unleashed the persecution of the Church under President Calles were the declarations of Monsignor Mora y del Río, Archbishop of Mexico, to a reporter from the newspaper *Universal*. He was protesting the articles of 1917, which converted what was called "freedom" into farce for Mexican Catholics. In fact, they took away all protection for priests, and they made the practice of the Catholic religion a crime. Soon after that the "Calles Law" was issued. This law was printed in fairly legible type and was posted on the main doors of all the churches. This had already been anticipated since during a stormy century there were signs of the coming of this particular storm. And finally, this religious persecution was unleashed by the Nero of the present century, President Plutarco Elías Calles, who governed the country from 1924 to 1928.

In this brief story one can appreciate the Spirit which lives in, guides, enlightens and strengthens the women of my Mexico. In that sad and terrible moment of our history, many heroic women rose up to fight for freedom of worship. There is a book that calls them the "Mexican Judiths." "It was charming and inspiring," says the book, "to see them with smiles on their faces and great courage delivering money and encouragement to the imprisoned priests; others offered their houses to hide them, not only the priests, but also the sisters and other persecuted people. Others braved even greater danger by taking in homeless people and unbaptized children, and they celebrated Mass and the sacraments in their homes (this was most dangerous, and was how they caught many priests whom they beat, tortured, and killed)." My mother, some aunts and other women, while saying the prayers of the Mass at the same time they believed it was being celebrated in some other place, were surprised by some soldiers (most certainly because of an informer) and arrested, beaten, and jailed for days. They had to witness how a group of nuns were beaten and stripped amidst jokes and laughter. Among them was their mother superior, a woman some ninety years old. What moved my mother most was the gentleness with which the nuns took so much mistreatment. The souls of these women who offered up their lives and suffering were indeed great.

In my mother's mind a sublime, holy and just ideal was awakened: the freedom of our Catholic Church, the soul and life of the Mexican nation. "To defend and preserve this sacred and charitable religion," we said, "is the most worthy and noble task that any well raised Mexican can accept, in spite of the ungrateful who have forgotten that which is most beautiful in our tradition and culture." In these events we can see that the one who loves, by the simple act of loving, opens a fountain of heavenly light in the heart.

When you sent me the papers inviting me to write, I went immediately to a priest with whom I've had a wonderful friendship for sixteen years. I showed him the papers and asked him what I should write in relation to what you were asking me. He answered me saying: "Clotilde, what they are asking is that you write about how God is present in your daily life. And about how you see, discover and teach about God every day. Start thinking and writing about what you do and have done for years."

I thought about it, but oh, is it hard to talk about oneself! I began with my childhood and the two stories—to show in a limited way the roots of my religion and culture. Moving on to another period of my life, I must admit the reason for my having immigrated to this country was that upon the death of my husband, his brother and partner in various businesses left us out in the cold. Two of my daughters were living in Salinas, California, and when they found out about my situation, they made arrangements for me to come live with them. We arrived on February 22, 1960, and as I said at the beginning, the culture shock was terrible. Everything seemed so strange to me: another language, another culture, different traditions. Homesickness caused a deep depression in me. At home and kneeling in front of Christ on the cross in church, I prayed tearfully that God would allow me to return to my country and would rid me of the hatred I felt for my brother-in-law and of the desire I had for the money that he kept. In God's infinite kindness, the request that was most important for my own good was granted. I no longer hate my brother-in-law Ignacio, nor do I covet his wealth, because now I am richer than he is. I have faith, freedom from those chains and the presence of Christ in my life. Nevertheless my homesickness for my people overwhelmed me for a long time.

On a three-day retreat I discovered God in my life, and an awareness that from my first steps he had guided me. There they told me that sometimes the Lord prunes us and transplants us, and it is there where we have to flower and bear fruit. That night I prayed: "Lord, I'm beginning to understand

that you want something from me. That's why you pulled me
up by the roots from that soil and you took away everything
that would prevent me from flowering and bearing fruit. Great
are you, my Lord, to those whom you call for your service in
your plan of salvation.''

At the close of that retreat, they gave me a cross and told
me: "Christ is counting on you." When I answered: "And I
on him," I gave my word and he gave his that this was how
it would be. That moment was sublime! The retreat director
presented me the little book *Camino* with this dedication:

> Clotilde: Walk by the side of the Lord always and you will feel
> how lovely life is when the footsteps of Christ are on the road.
> Walk always in the path which this Pilgrim shows you.

It was there that I discovered that Christ lives and is present among us, that he is not a distant God. There he was speaking to me, drying my tears, but also sending me. I gave my
word and the promise is sacred: *to walk toward the Father,
through Christ and the help of the Holy Spirit, with the help of Mary
and all the saints carrying with me all my brothers and sisters.* This
is what is fundamentally Christian. This was another dedication which a dear friend from Gilroy, California, sent in a post-
card. She and Lupe Sánchez and her sister Carmen are all great
examples of holiness. I worked with them for eight years in
the Christian *cursillos*. That's how my great adventure as a committed Catholic Christian began, in the company of no less than
the Master and Lord of the world and my Church. How could
I resist, when the entire Gospel invites us to walk always without tiring. Christ left us a command, and he rarely used the
imperative. Nevertheless, before his ascension to heaven, he
used it with all the authority invested in him: "Go to the whole
world, announce the Good News to all of creation. Go and
make all people my disciples" (Matt 28:19; Mark 16:15).

The same Gospel teaches us that the adventure of being
a Christian is more than just going through life saying: "Lord,
Lord." In addition we must act (Matt 7:21). Act here and now.
It's not easy to follow Christ, as many of us well know. In every
road there are stones, crossroads, blows which pierce the heart
so deeply that they send us reeling. I have received some of
these, and it's always from loved ones.

There was one incident that made me want to distance myself from everything; I asked myself bitterly: "What good is my commitment? Enough is enough!" It turned out that for ten years I threw myself with great love into the service of the parish. I went to the camps of migrant workers and taught them catechism so that they could receive the sacraments, and in the same way I prepared four families in the city. In one of them, not even the grandmother was confirmed. Then, one year, some of us who were mothers decided to enter our daughters as candidates to be Queen during the National Holidays of Mexico. We did it to raise money to pay off the debt from building the church; for years there was only enough to pay the interest. It was very, very hard work. However, I had the pleasure of giving $5,000.00 to the parish priest. I don't know how much the others turned in. It is impossible to tell here everything I did for my parish, for the priest, and for the community. I'm not trying to show off what I did, but only what happened to me and how God doesn't abandon me.

One Thursday afternoon, after Mass, the priest exposed the Blessed Sacrament and said to the people: "We're going to ask the Lord's pardon for the sins of people who have . . . ." (and he said everything that I had done or was doing). The only thing missing was to say my name. And he added: "They are nothing but whited sepulchres." At the foot of the Blessed Sacrament, there was a married couple invited by him, and in their prayer they said the same thing!

I never knew his motive, and though I asked many times that he see me, he never did. The priest is now dead. That couple always avoided me. I've now overcome my anger, but the pain that it caused me was very great. So great that my first thought was to quit everything. I entered into a tremendous struggle with myself. It was me against my faith, but my faith won. I cried out bathed in tears: "Lord, save me because I'm sinking" (Matt 14:30). This cry is always on my lips when I feel that I'm sinking in a sea of troubles. Nevertheless, I never drown because he is there, my Christ, giving me a hand, keeping me afloat. That's why I always say to groups both large and small:

> Let us walk always, carrying these great supplies in our pilgrim's knapsack: faith, hope and charity. We can find many hungry

people. Christ, incarnate love, declares: "I am the Way, the Truth, and the Life. No one comes to the Father except through Me" (John 14:6).

This is the idea that sustains me. It doesn't matter that I might still have to bleed. He "is my Shepherd, there is nothing that I want, his rod and his staff protect me," says the psalmist. I keep walking because he walks with me. I arrived in Chicago one winter seventeen years ago. I found it very cold. One Sunday, with the temperature below zero, I went out to look for a church and I found the parish of the Epiphany. Oh my God! I met Monsignor Hayes, a man who is all kindness. He has a great gift with people and the gift of holiness. I was able to count on his support in everything. And it is here that I embarked upon the most beautiful adventure of my life, giving myself tirelessly to others. The world is in agony not only because of the hunger for bread but also the hunger for peace and justice. This is the thing that keeps me from forgetting the great responsibility that I have. That is why I go from place to place, participating in everything I can. I can also say that none of it is just because of me. It is, first of all, because of God and, secondly, because of a great many people.

Together Fr. James Kiley and I initiated some lovely things and organized them with the participation of many others in the community. He arrived there very young and with a tremendous enthusiasm for working. He was always present in liturgies, meetings, social gatherings, and outings. I remember him because we shared all of this. He never excluded me for being old. His successor, Fr. Kevin Feeney, has been a great friend to me and to everyone. He was always with us in everything. How these two priests motivated us with their example of commitment!

I read in some book: "Spirituality is Christ in us." Therefore it is a spring that flows and flows without ever going dry. For eleven years I've had under my care a group of friends from the third stage of life. In each one, I truly see a wellspring of tenderness and generosity that never runs dry, a wellspring of inexhaustible faith in God, love for our Blessed Mother of Guadalupe, and a great love and respect for priests. It's a blessed age in which there's not much that can bother us. It's a blessed age because while the young are searching for pleasure, we, the elderly, are searching for God. Life has taught us that this is the only thing that matters because his love is the only truth.

Father, I hope I haven't disappointed you with this. And to make you laugh a little bit, a story. They say that a man jokingly told this saying to his wife: "Man is at the head of creation." To which she replied while rubbing her hand on his head: "And woman is the crown on top of the head."

I remain always your faithful servant,
Clotilde

Conclusions[1]

Writing about one's spirituality can be an arduous task. It was certainly a soul searching, vulnerable, stretching experience for each of our authors. Through their willingness to share something of their journeys into holiness and to speak of their relationships with God, these women and men become our teachers. They teach us that we, too, are enrolled in the school of life and have similar tales to share about the God who is revealed in the ordinary people and events of our lives.

It is not our purpose here to critique or analyze what has been written. We treat respectfully what has been offered to us so freely and honestly. Yet, we also admit that these stories have raised many questions for us. Two, in particular, intrigue us. They are: ''Are there any common elements that thread their way throughout these stories?'' and, ''What do these stories reveal about the uniqueness of an Hispanic spirituality?''

Journeying across Borders

One common element that weaves through these stories is the image of journey. This theme of movement, pilgrimage, dislocation and relocation is not new to those of us who are rooted in the Judaeo-Christian experience. Our journey finds resonance in the biblical narratives of the Israelites, God's chosen people, as they made their way from Egypt into the promised land. The Book of Exodus recounts Israel's successes, struggles and infidelities, while also chronicling Israel's growth in love and faithfulness to the ever faithful God. It was not so much Israel's journey into an unknown land, but their symbolic journey into the covenant that made them special before

God. Fr. Virgilio Elizondo similarly frames our understanding of the Hispanic experience in terms of a symbolic journey[2]—a journey into an unknown land, but also a symbolic journey from oppression to liberation by the grace of an ever faithful God. Journey or exodus is a valuable spiritual image for Hispanics and a privileged way of thinking about relationship to God, society and each other. We are *el pueblo de Dios en marcha* (the people of God on the move). Another way to understand the journey of Hispanics is to think of it in terms of "crossing borders."[3] Some borders are geographic, like a river separating one country from another. There are also cultural and social borders that confront us when we come to a new land with foreign customs, unusual foods and even different ways of participating in large gatherings. Then there are the borders of faith that conversion calls us to cross if we desire to experience Church, religion and worship in new ways. People cross identity borders on the way to personal integrity. Many Hispanics struggle to cross the borders of economic oppression in an effort to establish themselves in jobs, trades and households.

Our authors identified many kinds of journeys in their lives, with various types of borders that needed to be crossed. These can be revisited under the four subheadings of (1) relationships, (2) crisis moments, (3) feelings of God's presence, and (4) memories of root experiences.

Relationships: The family is at the heart of the Hispanic experience. The immediate family includes parents, siblings, grandparents, aunts, uncles, and cousins. We discover who we are through our family relationships. The school of life begins here. This is where faith is both taught and caught. We first know God through the love modeled and nurtured in the family. This includes the extended family as well, that is, *compadres* and *comadres*,[4] *concuños*,[5] and *tocayos*.[6]

Our writers illustrate how significant family members—living and deceased—have been in their lives, helping them to journey far and cross many borders. Marco Antonio López Saavedra's mother, for example, told him stories of the deceased members of his family. Even though Marco Antonio had never met his grandmother, he shares the family's sense of her closeness. His mother's heart warming stories about his grandmother Natividad helped him to know death as something familiar and not to be feared. The relationship with his deceased grandmother helped him deal with loss and pain as his own father crossed the threshold of death. Juan Sosa, on the other hand, writes in part about family gatherings and how these moments help him to remain rooted and schooled in the traditions of his own *familia*. For Hispanics, the family not only helps us to cross unfamiliar borders, but also to journey back to the beginnings that yet sustain us.

María Teresa Gastón Witchger found that her relationship with people outside her extended family, especially companions from Bread for the World and the Catholic Worker movement, inspired her to work for the rights of the poor. It was the relationship to the wider community that also enabled Olga Villa Parra and Ricardo to build their relationship on a commitment to justice for their Hispanic sisters and brothers. Ada María Isasi Díaz summarizes this journey when she writes, ''Drawing closer to God and struggling for justice have become one and the same for me.'' Here the journey is from an individualistic spirituality to a spirituality rooted in a relationship with family and the wider community, and justice is its name.

Our God language also seems to demonstrate a strong familiar relationship with the Holy One. When Hispanics feel gratitude we spontaneously say ''Dios se lo pague'' (''May God reward you''). When taking leave of someone we say ''Adios'' (''May God go with you''). Consuelo Covarrubias recalls that whenever her mother made plans or contemplated a new action, she instinctively said ''Si Dios nos da licencia'' (''If God wills it''). For Hispanics there is an unconscious crossing of sacred borders in everyday conversations. The very language we use in the ordinary school of life gives evidence of an intimacy with God, predicated upon the implicit belief that God has crossed the border into our lives.

Crisis Moments: How can we experience joy unless we have journeyed into pain? Hispanics' status as a minority means that they are constantly struggling to cross the borders of acceptance and equality within the political, economic, cultural and ecclesiastical worlds in which they live. This struggle is one of the teachers in our school of life, which reminds us that the crises, inner clashes, and suffering that arise out of family and community relationships hold seeds of promise and new life: if only we are willing to make the journey into God's providence. When Hispanics experience crisis, we instinctively attempt to relate such moments to God's providence. We know God has a plan for us, but we don't always understand where that plan will lead. When crises arise, we look for God to give meaning to the suffering, and to offer direction for resolution and redemption. Often it is a family member or friend who helps us discover God's plan and promise in our pain.

In our collection of very personal stories, José Rivera describes how he and Mercedes distanced themselves from God: the result, as they perceive it, was the disintegration of their marriage. Their actions were a great cross for their daughters and had a disastrous effect on their son. It was, in turn, their love for their son that helped them to learn surrender and trust in God. Together they crossed the border of division and pain to a new family unity and joy. Confesor de Jesús chronicled a number of crises in his life. One of the most painful was the rejection he felt from a group of companions whom he expected would understand him the most. His journey through each crisis left him with a deeper awareness and experience of God's unconditional love. Only when he let go and allowed the Lord to guide and befriend him was he able to be at peace. The spiritual paradox of letting go, of Christian abandonment in the Hispanic sense of *resignarse,* is what enables us to cross these sometimes painful borders.

Feelings of God's Presence. Hispanic peoples tend to live out of their hearts, not out of their heads. We will more often tell you what we feel than what we think. As Father Elizondo comments, for Hispanics "emotions are not seen as irrational but as complementary . . . to the whole person. . . . The heart is the center of the dynamic personality and has reasons the mind does not know."[7] This is especially true in our experience of God, whose presence is not abstractly imagined, but felt.

How often in our stories the authors have written about feeling or sensing the presence of God. Such feelings are important teachers in our everyday school of spirituality. Silvia Zaldívar uses the word *sentir* (to feel, to sense) when describing Hispanics' relationship with God. "When we sense God as Creator and Redeemer in our lives, we feel the need and the desire to adore . . . God." Such feelings helped Silvia to realize how God had journeyed into her life, and how she is invited to reciprocate by making the journey into God. This journey often takes place through popular devotions and worship which, in turn, evoke feelings of God's tangible presence among us. Feelings are key elements in this journey, helping us to cross over into a new consciousness and deeper awareness of the Lord in our lives.

Similarly, Yolanda Tarango recognized God in the faces of the poor and suffering when she acknowledged the feelings of pain and sadness that stirred in her as she lived among them. A new form of prayer or "presencing" God—feeling God's presence—emerged in her life. When she claimed her feelings, she crossed over from a style of institutionalized prayer to one that became integrated into her daily experiences, her work, but especially in living and working among the suffering and dispossessed.

Memories of Root Experiences: Ricardo Ramírez often remarks that the events we remember as pivotal in our lives are spiritually influential. Remembering or *hacer memoria* is a privileged way in which we cross over to a renewing experience of the sacred, of life as valuable, of the liberating power that comes from admitting and accepting our origins and our roots. The invitation to write about their spiritual journeys was a way for our authors to remember and to retell their root experiences of their relationships with God. In Ricardo's own story, he describes how the visit to Tía Petra's house during the family novena to Our Lady of Guadalupe lingers as his earliest memory of the sacred. He was surrounded by people and by those special objects that are the hallmarks of popular Catholicism: the *altarcito,* candles and pictures. The novena was a living lesson of faith that disposed him to sense a special presence of God on his way home. Dominga Zapata underscores the importance of recalling root experiences as she describes her own struggle to find an authentic spirituality. She represents so many Hispanics who have had to rediscover their roots . . . a rediscovery that not only feeds us culturally but also spiritually. For many of us, to become an authentically spiritual person means embracing our roots.

Alvaro Dávila affirms this in a very poignant way by noting, ''it seems like one's spiritual experience can only be known, contemplated and understood when we live in continuous dialogue with the memories of our People.'' He writes of his persistent denial of all that reminded him of his roots. He tells of the violence to self and the loss of human dignity that he experienced, unconscious though it may have been, while living a life of negation. His story reveals the painful price he paid for denying his roots. The very experience of writing as an exercise in memory provided the impetus to cross the border into a new awareness of the value and the wonder of his origins. Being in dialogue with our cultural roots is an important lesson in our school of spirituality.

We have attempted to look respectfully at these stories of spiritual journey. This is the way it should be, since these are stories of real people whose diverse journeys are a rich source of reflection. They demonstrate how Hispanics are a people who cross many boundaries, obstacles and divides in our journey to God. These stories represent something of the ethnic variety that exists within the Hispanic community and a few of the many borders that we cross. They also underscore a remarkable unity of vision and faith that binds us together. Many more stories need to be written, told and remembered.

The Final Story: An Oasis

To conclude, we return to the point where all Christian schools of spirituality begin: Jesus. Our spiritual Master said, ''The kingdom of God is like. . . .'' (Matt 13:24-53). It was up to those who heard these words to see what the Lord had in mind and to feel what he had in his heart so that they, in turn, might be able to discover in their minds and hearts what he was trying to teach them. Liturgist Mark Searle captured something of this in his frequent remark that ''the liturgy is a rehearsal of the kingdom.'' Liturgy is where people gather to ritualize the Lord's life, death and resurrection as each has seen, heard and felt it in their own lives. Yet, if the liturgy is a rehearsal of the kingdom, then could we not say that spirituality is the heartbeat of the kingdom? Spirituality is the energy that pulsates within us, giving meaning to all that we do in the Lord's name, and enabling us to cry out "Abba" in so many different languages, gestures, songs and religious practices. Spirituality is the energy that continually enables us to see what the Lord had in mind and to feel what he had in his heart so that we might discover again how "The kingdom of God is like . . ." an oasis.

The day's first light over the horizon illuminated the landscape for the three weary travelers—one woman and two men— who saw the silhouette of a palm tree in the distance. The tree appeared to be a promising place of refreshment from their very long journey, and the end of their common pilgrimage. As they grew closer, this trio of travelers noted that three others, at first hidden by the receding night, were seated under the tree. The trio watched as they stood, bid each other farewell, and moved off in different directions.

The travelers approached the place marked by the tree with a feeling of reverence for the refreshment they would soon enjoy. The trio, almost in silence, sipped the cool water and washed their dirty faces in the spring that sounded the message of welcome. In the early morning light they, like the three others before them, gathered under the palm tree to rest and await the day's providence.

As the sun moved through the sky, different people approached the oasis throughout the day. Each took their turn at the spring and then, with the original trio, sat under the palm. During this respite, each new guest began to tell her or his story. It was the story of how he or she had come to this moment. It was the story of the borders each had crossed, of the changes each had made, and of the healing each had known. The original three pilgrims became part of each new storyteller's words, felt the feelings behind the words, and entered into the story. After each tale was finished, the four sojourners breathed a deep, deep sigh. Eventually the guest, sufficiently rested, took leave of the trio, and left them waiting for another traveler and another story. How natural were the meetings that took place throughout that day. Many lifetimes moved through the oasis that day. As the last of these took their leave and faded into the distance, the sun too faded, leaving the trio in darkness with only the shimmer of the moon to help them discern one another's presence and the meaning of the day's events.

"Todo es hecho por Dios" ("Everything is made for God") became the spontaneous mantra that the three began to sing, to pray in the quiet of the night. In their singing a fourth voice was heard, harmonizing with their melody. It sang their song with gentle variations, and the night embraced their song. In the singing, the three began to see and feel what the storytellers had left them. Various apparitions paraded before them—not of the storytellers themselves, but of the One Presence whose voice now harmonized with their own as in the moonlit night. "Todo es hecho por Dios" took on new meaning in the unfolding of their night song. They were the same, and yet they were different. Their own stories now flowed from them as naturally as those of the other pilgrims throughout the day. The Presence, whose voice now overshadowed their own, revealed that it is in the telling that all are part of a greater story, of a greater hymn, of a greater and more resplendent Presence. And so night passed, the music faded, and the day dawned. The woman and the two men stood in the rising sun, knowing that their pilgrimage was ended. Like the three strangers before them, they embraced in a final farewell and moved off in different directions. In the distance, there appeared faint images of three other travelers who moved toward the palm and its promise of refreshment.

The Lord simply and profoundly teaches us that our uniqueness in the Spirit arises in the religious traditions, the cultural rituals and the practices of faith that unfold the Presence that we call God. We three pilgrims—Arturo, Consuelo, and Ed—and you with us, have seen throughout these pages that the Presence was experienced in a well, a novena, an image, the poor, one's family, and in so many other simple yet significant ways. These experiences changed the storytellers. Each of them emerged from the encounter transformed and moved in a new direction.

The experience of God cannot be defined as much as it can be narrated. The same is true of spirituality, elusive as a heartbeat and best captured in a story. Whatever is unique about Hispanic spirituality is caught and taught in the telling of a tale. Similar to the Kingdom, "Hispanic spirituality is like. . . ." The uniqueness of this spirituality comes in the way life is accepted as a parable, played out in the faith images of popular religion—popular Catholicism. Efforts to explain and define Hispanic spirituality are never very successful. Yet we must try, because the effort to do so itself affirms anew the experience of God in our lives.

Though very diverse, Hispanics are able to enter into each other's parable if and when we embrace popular forms of Catholicism as a source of our own spirituality—if and when we come to the oasis, refresh our weary lives, and tell our stories to one another. Hispanics who have consciously distanced themselves from their roots or who have not had the opportunity to be in personal contact with the potent images of their history are also invited to this oasis. They are invited to drink from the wellspring of this life through the baptisms and weddings, funerals and other familial and community gatherings. At such moments, immersed in popular faith images and ritual practices, something is awakened in us, and we are propelled into the story. And once inside we begin to understand how the story and the parable create a longing for more, a desire for companionship, a passion for truth. Parables create a longing for God.

What we have heard and felt in this book is an invitation into the parable. We have experienced a lesson from the school of Hispanic spirituality, the heartbeat of the kingdom, as it pulsates in our community. *Así es!*

NOTES

1. The editors are grateful to Fr. John Telles, Ms. Sally Teresa Kelley, and Sr. Margarita Armendariz for their encouragement and for their special assistance in shaping these conclusions.

2. See especially his *Galilean Journey* (Maryknoll: Orbis Books, 1991). Although Elizondo writes from a specifically Mexican-American perspective, his work offers a framework for understanding the physical and spiritual pilgrimage of other Hispanic groups as well.

3. Arturo Bañuelas, "U.S. Hispanic Theology," unpublished paper.

4. These are the godparents, who not only have spiritual responsibilities, but whose relationships have social and political ramifications for the family as well.

5. The relationship between married siblings.

6. Those who have the same name.

7. Virgilio Elizondo, *Christianity and Culture* (San Antonio: Mexican-American Cultural Center Publications, 1975) 166–67.

Contributors

Ada María Isasi-Díaz, Cuban, associate professor of theology and ethics at Drew University and author on Hispanic women's spirituality, has recently published *En La Lucha* (1993), where she elaborates a *mujerista* theology.

Yolanda Tarango, C.V.V.I., Mexican-American, past coordinator of Las Hermanas, U.S.A., and currently on the Incarnate Word sisters leadership team, is coauthor with Ada María Isasi-Díaz of the book *Hispanic Women: Prophetic Voice in the Church* (1988).

Alvaro Dávila, Guatemalan, associate director of the Instituto de Liderazgo Pastoral and pastoral associate of Our Lady of Mercy Parish, both in Chicago, is a lecturer and a great animator of groups in Hispanic ministry.

Dominga M. Zapata, Puerto Rican, of the Society of Helpers, the Hispanic-American consultant for the Ethnic Ministries Office of the Archdiocese of Chicago, is a doctoral candidate at the University of Salamanca, Spain.

Consuelo Covarrubias, P.B.V.M., Mexican-American, in Hispanic ministry, coordinates the Small Christian Communities for the Diocese of Gary, Indiana, pastors Hispanics at Sacred Heart Parish, Michigan City, and shares the roots of her spirituality as a religious woman.

Ricardo Ramírez, C.S.B., Mexican-American, bishop of the Diocese of Las Cruces, New Mexico, has written and published many articles, among them notable ones on Hispanic spirituality and on Hispanic popular religiosity.

Juan Sosa, Cuban, director of worship for the Archdiocese of Miami, shares his experience of spirituality as an Hispanic diocesan priest.

María Teresa Gastón Witchger, mother of three, former member of the national Youth Task Force, former youth minister, currently works with migrant women in Immoklee, Florida.

Marco Antonio López Saavedra, Mexican-American, former pastoral associate at Epiphany Parish and currently on the faculty of Niles College Seminary, Chicago, writes of his spirituality from the perspective of youth.

Olga Villa Parra, Mexican-American, on the staff of the Lilly Foundation of Indianapolis, brings the rich story of her spirituality as a married Hispanic woman who has been immersed as leader and companion to her Latino community for years.

José and *Mercedes Rivera,* Salvadorans, directors of the Movimiento Familiar Católico, U.S.A., work with Marriage Encounter and Pre-Cana and share deeply of their life story and how it has formed their spirituality as a married couple.

Enrique D. Alonso, Mexican, past coordinator for Continuing Education and Retreats for ordained deacons and current director of the Instituto de Liderazgo for Hispanic, is deacon at Our Lady of Grace Parish in Chicago.

Confesor De Jesús, Puerto Rican, deacon at St. Sylvester's and past teacher at Loyola University, Chicago, on Hispanic spirituality brings his experience as a divorced person and how it has transformed the spirituality in his daily life.

Silvia Zaldívar, Cuban, member of the national Catholic Convening on Aging representing the Minority Advocacy Committee on Catholic Charities and on the Illinois Council of Aging, writes of her experience with her peers and their struggles as they grow in their spirituality.

Clotilde Olvera Márquez, Mexican, (R.I.P.) foundress of the Sagrada Family, P.C.E.B., for Hispanic Elderly in Little Village community, thoroughly involved in parish life at Epiphany, Chicago, wrote movingly of experiences from childhood as an immigrant of those profound moments of grace that deepened life with God.

Arturo Pérez, Mexican, priest of the Archdiocese of Chicago, writes and lectures on Hispanic popular Catholicism.

Edward Foley, Capuchin, teaches at Catholic Theological Union in Chicago.